Equal Partners

HOW TO BUILD A LASTING RELATIONSHIP

TINA B. TESSINA & RILEY K. SMITH

Headway · Hodder & Stoughton

WE DEDICATE THIS BOOK
TO OUR GODDAUGHTER
AMANDA HALLEY BIALACK,
AGE SEVEN, WHO HOPEFULLY
WILL GROW INTO A WORLD
WHERE HEALTHY RELATION-
SHIPS, BASED ON MUTUAL
CO-OPERATION AND RESPECT,
ARE THE NORM.

Cataloguing in Publication Data is available from the British Library

ISBN 0 340 602775

First published in US by The Putnam Publishing Group, 1993
First published by Hodder Headline, 1994
Impression number   10 9 8 7 6 5 4 3 2 1
Year   1998 1997 1996 1995 1994

Typeset by Wearset, Boldon, Tyne and Wear
Printed in Great Britain for Hodder & Stoughton Educational, a division of Hodder Headline Plc, 338 Euston Road, London NW1 3BH by Thomson Litho Ltd.

CONTENTS

Preface   iv

Chapter 1   Equal Partners   1

Chapter 2   Define And Communicate Your Problem   18

Chapter 3   Agree To Negotiate   42

Chapter 4   Set The Stage   87

Chapter 5   State Your Wants   102

Chapter 6   Explore Your Options And Decide   118

Chapter 7   Creating Equal Partnership   139

Useful Addresses   151

PREFACE

*I*f you are struggling to find lasting satisfaction in your intimate relationships, you're not alone. Like the many couples we have worked with, you may be struggling with your partner, searching for a way to be happy together:

- you may have experienced a sequence of relationships that were destructive and didn't work;
- you may be with someone new and fear you will repeat old, painful patterns;
- you may have a basically good relationship with some specific problems (financial struggles, disagreement about parenting, sex, housework or time schedules) that you can't find a satisfactory solution for. Or,
- you may fight all the time, unable to resolve even minor family problems or conflicts without a painful and exasperating struggle, which leaves one or both of you feeling hurt, angry, resentful, deprived, cheated or frustrated.

If so, you're not alone. Most people have trouble sustaining a long-term, intimate relationship with a partner.

EMPHASISING THE POSITIVE

*M*uch has been written about relationship problems in recent years, including many books with an emphasis on unhealthy relationships, such as relationships with alcoholics, compulsive or obsessive love, domestic violence and sexual molestation. These books have focused on the emotional and psychological (and often physical) damage these relationships cause, how to recognise them and how to break free from them. Simply recognising, describing and suggesting ways to end these problems is an enormous task.

All of these books focus on unsatisfying or unhealthy relationship patterns and how to recognise and overcome them. Little is said about how to create and sustain a healthy, functional, non co-dependent relationship. You may be very familiar with the frustration of being told how not to do it but not really ever understanding what to do instead.

So, if you're asking, 'What is a healthy, functional relationship and how do I get one?' *Equal Partners* is designed to answer your questions and teach you (either individually or together with your partner) how to create and sustain a fully functioning partnership between equals.

Equal Partners is a workbook that provides partners with a proven, step-by-step guide for working together as a team. You can learn to overcome negative relationship patterns and master the positive new skills you'll need to know to create a successful, satisfying and sustainable relationship that fulfils the individual needs of both you and your partner.

Equal Partners is a guideline for transforming an unsatisfying relationship into a loving, sustainable, healthy partnership between equals who support each other and work together co-operatively to ensure that each partner gets what he or she wants. We call this equal, mutually supportive relationship an *equal partnership*.

At the centre of *Equal Partners* is a method for *co-operative problem solving*, which involves both of you working together as a team. Through this process, any problems, difficulties, obstacles, differences or struggles that arise can be identified, negotiated and solved to the mutual satisfaction of you and your partner.

This book will lead you, individually and together, through a series of carefully planned exercises designed to help you develop the skills (such as problem solving, co-operation, clear communication and teamwork) that will enable you to use the co-operative problem solving process to build and sustain a healthy relationship.

In *Equal Partners* you will learn how to work together smoothly to solve the very problems that created competition, pain and conflict between you and your partner in the past and build teamwork and co-operation where you previously had fighting, frustration and despair. Your problems are probably solvable; relationship problems feel overwhelming and difficult only if the partners involved lack the skills they need to solve them.

The core concept for co-operative problem solving is *the negotiation tree* – a step-by-step guide to working smoothly together to solve all the problems and disputes partners can encounter in the course of a relationship. It will guide you safely through the five steps of solving any problem and help the two of you reach a solution that is wholly satisfying to both of you.

Equal Partners will introduce you to a relationship of equality:

- designed to meet your unique needs as individuals and as a couple;
- in which both you and your partner feel equally important, equally powerful, equally free to express wants and needs;
- where both you and your partner work together to find a mutually satisfactory way to get what both of you want every single time;
- where you support each other in making sure you both are satisfied in the relationship;
- which contains far less conflict, frustration, anger and fewer arguments, disputes and feelings of deprivation than most couples experience; and
- which is easy to sustain because you both learn how to get what you want from it all the time!

A FOCUS ON BUILDING RELATIONSHIPS THAT WORK

*I*n the last few years, there has been a growing focus on self-defeating relationship patterns: poor communication, competition, chronic self-denial and unequal power, which lead to dissatisfaction and dissension between partners. This awareness has come about through the discovery that a large percentage of relationships fail to function well or fail altogether. You probably know more couples that are having trouble or are divorced than couples who are successful. Today, couples are divorced as often as other couples are married. You may have had more failed than successful relationships yourself.

Relationships fail so often because we rarely get a chance to learn the necessary skills for healthy relationships. Personal issues are not discussed in school and parents either don't understand or don't discuss their intimate relationship issues with us. Even marriage counsellors tend to focus on the individual's problems rather than couple skills. So most of us learned what we know about relationships by the example of those around us, who often fought, split up or were dishonest with each other, and through media images, which displayed unrealistically happy and harmonious couples or dramaticised infidelity, addiction, fighting and passion. These models have presented us with little useful information about how to form a healthy working partnership between equals.

These images and examples naturally focus us on what's wrong, but the effective way to remedy the problems is to focus on what works.

The study of psychology, especially in relationships, is a relatively new science and, as with most new fields of study, it focused on the areas of relationships that created pain and trouble. Not until psychologists found ways of alleviating the pain and eliminating destructive behaviours and began to find some solutions, did we begin to focus on what the healthy models are.

Equal Partners will teach you effective skills and techniques that work. While this book will help you discover many of the ineffective ways of working together that have turned your past problem-solving efforts into tense, conflict-filled sessions, its main focus is on teaching you new behaviours and attitudes that will help you create a relationship that does work. To do this, you do not need to delve deeply into your personal, emotional history or problems, or wait until they are all corrected; instead, all you need to do is learn new skills and approaches to solving relationship problems.

In our own personal experience, and the experiences of our clients and students, we realised that most people were attempting to follow models for relationships that had no relationship to their own personalities, needs, lifestyles and preferences. Instead they used relationship models learned from their parents, from television, books and films, or from observations and assumptions about the relationships of others around them. Because these models were from other times and places, and based on the needs, prejudices, preferences and personalities of others, they felt awkward, stifling and dissatisfying and didn't work. In short, the models were impossible to sustain.

What was needed was a method of developing a 'custom-made' relationship, one that so well suited the people involved and came naturally enough to them, that they felt satisfied and motivated to sustain it.

Over a decade ago we began writing and leading workshops that helped couples discover how two people willing to treat each other as equals can have a satisfying, committed life together.

HOW THE WORKBOOK IS ORGANISED

The first chapter, Equal Partners, explains what an intimate partnership between equals is, why it works so well, and how you can achieve it. Co-operative problem solving is also introduced and explained, as well as the negotiation tree. The tree will outline and guide you through the five steps of the process, referring you back to the proper information and exercises whenever you have difficulty and helping you to know when you are ready to go on to the next step.

The next five chapters correspond to the steps of the negotiation tree: Define and Communicate Your Problem; Agree to Negotiate; Set the Stage; State Your Wants; and Explore Your Options and Decide.

These chapters explain each step and give information, exercises and guidelines that teach you skills for overcoming each problem as it arises. All these chapters present examples of couples engaged in negotiating to demonstrate how your new skills will work.

The last chapter, Creating Equal Partnership, outlines ideas for using co-operative problem solving and the negotiation tree to improve various aspects of your relationship and thus, over a period of time, transform it into a relationship that is wholly satisfying to both of you. This will enhance your pleasure in being together and make your relationship easy to sustain.

USING THE EXERCISES

We recommend you begin by reading this book through in its entirety to gain an overview of the stages of the negotiation tree and the relationship skills that accompany them. You may be tempted to begin immediately by using the negotiation tree to solve a problem you are having, but if you do, you will probably find yourself feeling lost and frustrated because, without reading the rest of the book, you will not have enough understanding of what is meant by many of the suggestions and steps of the negotiation tree.

The exercises in *Equal Partners* are designed to teach every skill you'll need to develop and explore every barrier you may encounter in order to achieve a healthy relationship.

The exercises build on each other, with many of the later exercises drawing on skills you learned in the earlier ones. Each exercise is prefaced with a complete explanation of what it is designed to teach and when it might be needed in your relationship. Step-by-step instructions help make the exercises easy to follow and easy to do.

Because of the sequential nature of the exercises and because you will be building on the skills you learned in the earlier exercises, you will probably find that the skills you learn are easy to remember when you are involved in negotiation or interaction within your relationship.

Each exercise will give you criteria for determining when you have mastered each skill or deciding when you still need more practice. If you find you need help with certain skills or you need help at a particular point in your negotiation, the negotiation tree will refer you to the proper exercises and examples. At any time, you can pause in your negotiation long enough to go through an exercise needed to help you overcome any difficulty or confusion you're having and then return to the negotiation tree for the next step.

There are exercises you can do as an individual and exercises you can do with your partner. The exercises are given at the point when the skills they teach are needed in the co-operative problem solving process, so we recommend you do them in the order they are presented. The exercises themselves will refer you to other related exercises that might be helpful. We have designed this sequence to meet the needs of the broadest number of readers but each couple has individual negotiating strengths and weaknesses and the negotiation tree will help you adapt the guidelines and exercises to your own situation. Experiment with the negotiation tree, and, as you use it, you will see which techniques you and your partner most need and which guidelines are most helpful.

The negotiation tree is a negotiating roadmap to the five steps of co-operative problem solving Once you feel you understand the steps of the tree, the book will guide you to try using it on a simple practice problem. You and your partner will be astonished to discover how easy it is to use and you will both find a solution which satisfies you.

By the time you have mastered all the skills and exercises taught here, you will have a full set of tools that will enable you to resolve any problems that may arise in your relationship, *before* you and your partner are so frustrated and angry that your problem becomes too big to handle.

THIS BOOK IS FOR EVERYONE IN AN INTIMATE RELATIONSHIP

The authors of this book personally advocate no particular form or kind of intimate relationship. We recognise that there are as many valid and fulfilling kinds of relationships as there are different kinds of people. Instead of advocating rules and guidelines for how your relationship 'should' look, we teach you how to discover the unique requirements your individual relationship must meet in order to be sustainable and rewarding for you.

By reading this book, doing the exercises and following the negotiation tree, you will give yourself the best possible chance of creating a relationship you can both enjoy, feel proud to share and in which you will feel comforted and supported.

We invite you to turn the following pages and begin building your equal partnership.

CHAPTER 1

EQUAL PARTNERS

*I*n fifteen years of working with couples, we have found that when couples in difficulty present what they believe are unsolvable problems, a solution can always be found when we apply co-operative problem solving. Even when people came to us with the problem that had caused their divorce or breakup, we could find at least one solution acceptable to both of them. As experts in problem solving, we knew how to help each couple explore all their underlying needs, break free from old, problem-creating behaviours and eliminate the false limitations they had placed on the problem. We have found, repeatedly, that most of the trouble between intimate partners happens because they don't know how to work together to solve problems. The frustration, resentment, anger, disappointment and despair these couples feel almost always stems from not being able to get what they want from the relationship and from each other. Whether their fights are about money, sex, affection, time, infidelity, in-laws, raising children, housekeeping or other problems, their inability to reach a mutually agreeable or satisfying solution forces them to repeat the same old arguments, without any resolution. Or they remain locked in the habitual ways of relating that they think they should use but that create dissatisfaction and conflict between them.

As therapists, we spend much of the time teaching couples the skills they need to solve problems together successfully and teaching them how to work together as a team rather than struggle against each other. We also spend time guiding people through the process of problem solving, to keep them on the track and prevent them from sliding back into their old habits.

If you are like most of the people we counsel, you have probably entered relationships madly in love, convinced that your feelings for each other were so strong that they would carry you through into an equal partnership in which, as partners you would:

- give and take equally, with each partner feeling equally responsible and equally rewarded by the relationship;
- be committed to mutual satisfaction – if one of you is not happy, the other really wants to help solve the problem;
- face problems rather than avoid them, confident that you have a range of skills to resolve any disagreements, struggles and conflicts that occur;
- seldom have to compromise, because you work together so that both of you get what you want;

1

- feel like a team, working together to maximise your power, instead of competing and undercutting your collective efforts;
- treat each other's feelings, wants and needs as important;
- share thoughts and feelings freely, knowing that positive interaction adds energy to the relationship and negative thoughts and feelings indicate a problem which you are confident you can solve together;
- encourage each other and recognise you need excitement as well as comfort and security;
- feel comfortable, satisfied and stimulated, so you have little incentive to seek out others or begin a new relationship;
- have confidence that your relationship will last, because problems are solved as they arise and not allowed to persist and linger until they breed resentment.

However, your relationship failed to live up to these dreams, because after a short time it ran into problems, which you did not know how to handle, like Carol and Paul.

CAROL AND PAUL

Carol and Paul were childhood sweethearts and married young, with the support of both families and a big celebration with all their friends. They had a dream relationship and high hopes for happiness. Now thirty-five and a working wife, Carol has spent most of her adult life taking care of others – especially Paul – but feels unworthy of *receiving* attention and doesn't realise that it is equally important to take care of herself. Meanwhile Paul, a thirty-eight-year-old blue-collar worker, has trouble showing affection, and since he isn't demonstrative and supportive towards Carol, she feels depleted and unresponsive towards him. It doesn't take long for them both to feel deprived and neglected, and their relationship becomes unsustainable. Neither of them can sustain their good feelings towards each other when they feel so deprived, yet both, being insecure, feel that the survival of their relationship depends upon maintaining their roles.

Like Carol and Paul and many others, you may have had a relationship that frequently felt more like a nightmare than a dream, and you may have found yourself and your partner struggling with individual wants and needs that differ, without knowing how to work together effectively to solve the conflict. The resulting frustration, anger and battles have made the relationships more and more unpleasant and difficult to sustain.

Many relationships we observe – our parents', our friends', on films and television – aren't working very well. They seem to be full of struggle, pain and boredom, and fraught with problems:

- one partner gives and the other takes;
- one is an addict, alcoholic or gambler and the other pays the price;
- one partner overpowers, coerces, defrauds, deceives or takes advantage of the other;
- they both follow rigid roles that seem to alter or stifle their personalities;

- one gives up a career to support a spouse who succeeds, then leaves;
- both partners seem filled with anger, contempt, hostility or hatred of the other;
- both compromise their needs for the survival of the marriage;
- they both withhold their true thoughts and feelings for fear of hurting their partner and feel dissatisfied;
- one or both are numb, depressed, or detached and are partners only in that they cohabitate, or they stay together for the sake of their children or because they feel they have to;
- the romance is gone and there is no vitality;
- their sexual needs and differences seem to conflict, creating emotional suffering for both; or
- one or both have affairs to fill a missing need in their partnership.

But there is hope. Co-operative problem solving can help you learn to work out mutually satisfactory solutions to problems like these, by working together to ensure each other's satisfaction. If the problem is too severe or long-standing to be solved by mutual discussion, co-operative problem solving will direct you to seek help, while simultaneously showing you how to make room in the relationship for individual differences, preferences and tastes.

You can have a successful, equal partnership even if either of you or both of you still have personal, emotional problems that are unresolved. Working together, you can help each other overcome individual problems (whether they are emotional, from past history, work-related or stem from some other part of your separate lives), and you can make enough room in your relationship for your moods and personalities to co-exist without undue struggle. As you develop more effective ways of mutual co-operation, your sense of inner equality will grow and further enhance your relationship, in an ever-increasing spiral.

Co-operative problem solving offers you an easy-to-follow, effective, non-competitive method to help you work together to:

- recognise and solve problems in your relationship, whether you've been together for a long time or you are a newly committed couple;
- prevent your individual problems from creating partnership problems;
- solve each others' individual problems to your mutual satisfaction;
- solve your relationship problems to your mutual satisfaction;
- review the interaction in your past relationships to learn what went wrong, identify behaviour and beliefs that got in your way before and correct them;
- identify old relationship patterns that were destructive, addictive or abusive, and develop healthy interaction;
- discuss changing or conflicting individual moods and feelings or different needs for intimacy, and find ways to accommodate them;
- identify and examine the traditional relationship models to see what aspects of them are relevant to your partnership and what you need to change;

- develop a model for partnership, no matter what your style, orientation or preference, that works for you both; and
- learn the skills you need to be whole, healthy, independent individuals who have satisfying, loving intimacy as equal partners.

DECISION MAKING: IT TAKES EQUALS TO SOLVE PROBLEMS

There is a pervasive myth that somehow happy couples just agree on everything automatically all the time. Because we believe this myth, we enter relationships convinced that whatever problems or differences we have with our partners will be easy to solve. But, in reality, the individuals who make up a partnership will disagree frequently and often struggle over even minor issues.

In the course of building and sustaining a lifetime relationship, we are bound to encounter many problems. Our different backgrounds and experience, our individual perception of each other and events, our unequal levels of education, our individual needs for self-expression and contact and our differing values and beliefs about relationships complicate and often block our attempts at problem solving. Compounding all this is the fact that models of healthy, effective problem solving between partners in a relationship have been rare or non-existent. For centuries, the accepted models for family, business and political relationships were patriarchal and authoritarian with a parental leader (usually male) in charge who made all the critical decisions and passed them down to subordinates (often female), who accomplished them without question.

Although competition may work in business, relationship models based on the idea that one person must lead and the other follow, one win and the other lose, become power struggles, where the partners fight bitterly when they disagree. They struggle to be in control or avoid disagreements altogether because they feel it isn't worth the struggle or they wouldn't win anyway. Hence they spend a lot of their time either fighting for what they want or feeling deprived. You may have witnessed your parents, friends or neighbours interacting in this way because, in the past, relationships like these have been the norm.

COMPETITION

The belief that someone has to win in a relationship encourages us to compete rather than to co-operate. As children we see a teacher favouring a brighter student, or a sister who is more aggressive deciding what game we'll play. The message is that if we aren't the best, don't fight hard or manipulate, we won't get what we want, which leads us to either struggle for it or give up.

Partners try to win, because in competition, only one person gets what they want. Most of us are used to competing for jobs, sports or dates and we even compete with ourselves to see if we can outdo our previous efforts. When competition is stimulating, motivating and fun, it is healthy.

Between partners, however, competition becomes stressful, counter-productive and toxic, poisoning the relationship by turning partners into adversaries and undermining the mutual support and encouragement vital to becoming equal partners.

FEAR OF DIFFERENCE

There is another reason we so often have difficulty resolving problems and conflicts with our intimate partners and handle them clumsily or even badly. In a relationship where we feel a deep bonding or sense of merged identity, we experience a strong tendency to perceive disagreements as threatening. Disagreeing seems to indicate to us that we are separate individuals who perceive everything differently and have different needs and wants, and we fear that we'll be rejected or disapproved of if we are different.

PROBLEMS OUTSIDE THE RELATIONSHIP

Sometimes relationship problems are only indirectly connected to your partnership: your car breaks down, your children need to get to school, your boss is difficult to get along with. These issues become partnership problems because you bring their effects, big and small, home (into the relationship) with you. Anger at your unreasonable boss can quickly result in a difficult evening with your partner if you bring your frustration home and are irritable, and the two of you end up arguing unnecessarily.

While this feels unfair and inappropriate, in real life it frequently happens. A couple unskilled in working together to solve problems could easily become tangled in a web of blaming, hurt and anger and, after years of similar unresolved conflicts, they can build a backlog of bitterness that can't be healed.

PROBLEMS WITHIN THE RELATIONSHIP

Sometimes problems are directly related to your relationship: you fight about housework or money, you have conflicts over sex. One or both of you becomes hurt or angry. At these times, if you have no method for co-operative negotiation, the conflict (and the resulting negative feelings) can easily escalate into a big problem or accumulate over time, because the problems cause friction and never get resolved, and undermine an otherwise loving and viable partnership.

Struggling with your partner and believing you can't both have what you want prevents you from co-operative problem solving. You may believe that you can't get what you want because:

- there isn't enough to go around;
- you don't deserve it as much as the other person;
- it will be taken away from you; or
- it isn't nice to want things.

When disagreements or difficulties arise, if you feel hopeless, panicked, angry or confused, you won't be able to think clearly enough to solve the problem.

EFFECTIVE DECISION MAKING

Only recently have psychologists and sociologists begun to discuss the elements of effective decision making. Among other discoveries, they found that decision making (even in business) is more effective when everyone contributes their views of priorities and their thoughts about possible solutions. This co-operative approach means that everyone contributes their understanding to the problem and everyone feels involved in the process and committed to the success of the solution they agree upon.

If, up to now, you viewed negotiation in a relationship as a struggle or a hassle, an opportunity to be overpowered or cheated, you are not alone. Because we live in a competitive society, it is difficult to realise that, when we are dealing with those we love, problems can be solved through co-operative teamwork, and that solutions can be reached where no one loses and everyone benefits.

In this book you will learn an effective new model for resolving the difficulties you will inevitably experience as a couple in a relationship. We call this approach *co-operative problem solving* and you may find it almost revolutionary. In co-operative problem solving, both parties attempting to resolve a conflict or make a decision involving them can negotiate so that both get what they want. The following chapters will help you learn all the highly affective decision-making skills you need to solve each relationship problem as it arises. You will learn how to solve the problems of the past (I'm afraid we'll argue about money like my first wife and I did); the present (I don't think you're doing your fair share of the housework); and the future (what will we do if I lose my job?). Instead of a struggle or something to avoid, solving problems will become an opportunity to reaffirm your mutual love and caring and strengthen your partnership and teamwork.

CO-OPERATIVE PROBLEM SOLVING

Co-operative problem solving means you solve problems by working together as equals, rather than struggling with each other, so all of your emotional, mental and creative energy can be focused on finding a solution, creatively exploring the problem, developing alternatives, putting your mutually chosen solutions into action and solving the problem.

You may think that's a lot to promise, because the idea that both of you can work together to get all that both of you want every time runs counter to conventional wisdom and perhaps your own personal experience.

Because our world offers few examples of co-operation, and many examples of competition, winning and losing, couples tend to approach problem solving in the same competitive way. When we want different things, we argue over which of us gets our way, insisting on our being 'right' or on making the other 'wrong' in order to have our way. Or we just give up, convinced it is not worth it or we can never win against our partner, and we feel restricted, deprived, hurt and angry. This is especially true in relationship problems.

Carol and Paul, for example, have a conflict. They both want the car for the evening. Because of their conflicting wants, they are anxious that there might not be enough transport for the two of them and begin arguing. Carol, after arguing for 20 minutes about who needs or deserves the car more, gets angry enough to grab the keys and take the car, leaving Paul to find other transport. Carol has 'won' the car but created a bigger relationship problem: Paul ends up feeling deprived and angry, Carol feels anxious and guilty. Because they are convinced there is no way both of them can have what they want, they get upset and quarrel. Neither of them considers an alternative solution, and someone has to do without transport.

On the other hand, if Carol and Paul learn co-operative problem solving, they will know how to work together as a team to reach a solution that is mutually satisfying. Confident that their goal is that *both* of them be content with the result, Carol and Paul will be much less likely to approach the transportation problem with a win or lose attitude, and both will find it much easier to be flexible, accepting and understanding of the other's position.

They consider other options: Paul can get a ride with a neighbour, relative or friend; Carol can drop Paul off on her way; either can take a taxi, bus or train; someone else may let them borrow a car; they can adjust their schedules so they don't need the car at the same time; or they might even decide to rent or buy another car. They can negotiate until they both are satisfied.

The negotiations you will learn in this book will not prove you're wrong and your partner is right, or vice versa, because the main purpose of co-operation is to avoid the competitive win/lose attitude which means that someone has to be wrong. These negotiations are based on the belief that both of you are right and deserve to have what you want.

At first, this co-operative approach may seem radically different and even foreign to you, but you will find it makes sense as it is presented in the negotiation tree, and is very effective. Like others who have used these ideas and exercises, you can create teamwork and equal partnership in your relationship.

By following the five steps of co-operative problem solving, you will learn a method of resolving conflict based on better understanding each other's wants and needs, communicating clearly, developing new, creative options, making decisions and reaching solutions that are completely satisfactory to both partners. It will help you master the basic attitudes and skills of co-operation at the same time as it helps you to solve your problems.

This way of thinking also motivates you and your partner to participate equally and actively in resolving struggles, because the goal is always to develop a solution that is completely satisfying to both of you. Co-operative problem solving minimises confusion by teaching you specific options, such as how to clarify and communicate the problem, how to make sure your partner is equally involved and what to do when your partner doesn't want to co-operate.

If you co-operate to solve problems when they arise, the experience of working together and caring about each other's wants (Paul and Carol mutually decide that Carol will drop Paul off, so they both have transportation) will build trust and goodwill between you. This feeling of mutual trust (the next negotiation about the car will be easier and Carol and Paul will be more relaxed because they co-operated this time) and confidence that you can successfully meet challenges together creates a solid bond between you and is the key to establishing an equal partnership.

Co-operative problem solving will help you solve problems:

- when you know what you want, but you're not getting it;
- when you and your partner seriously disagree, over what you want or how to handle a problem;
- each time you have a partnership decision to make, from buying a new car or house to deciding whose career move is most beneficial;
- if you know you're unhappy but aren't sure what you want;
- if your partner is obviously unhappy and you don't know why.

As you read through the chapters and do the exercises you and your partner will quickly see which negotiation problems arise most often for you, which skills you need to practise, and which attitudes have kept you stuck in your past relationship problems. As you practise the skills and follow the guidelines you will overcome barriers, correct old, competitive attitudes and develop new skills for communicating; problem solving will become easier and flow more naturally.

BARRIERS AND SKILLS

As you begin to learn and work with the five steps of the technique you will learn many new skills and probably encounter a number of difficulties that will tempt you to give up and abandon the process. We call the difficulties that arise the *barriers* to co-operative problem solving, and each chapter outlines the typical barriers (such as: not knowing what you want, competing, inexperience and mistrust, confusion, lack of communication, not enough information and unresolved anger) you are likely to encounter at each step of the process. Each chapter teaches you specific skills designed to overcome these barriers. For each barrier that arises, the negotiation tree will teach you and your partner the skills you need:

- to be aware of the possible barriers;
- to anticipate them and minimise the problems they cause; and
- to overcome the barriers you do encounter as you learn co-operative problem solving.

CO-OPERATION AND EQUAL PARTNERSHIP

*E*qual partnership is the long-range benefit of learning to problem solve in this way. After you and your partner have used co-operative problem solving to work together to resolve several problems in a totally satisfying way, you will begin to feel more secure about your teamwork and, therefore, your partnership. Knowing you can make agreements that both of you will keep and that when problems arise you can work together to solve them, will build a deeper level of trust between you – trust that you can handle life's difficulties, problems and disagreements in a spirit of co-operation, trust that you both are willing to work for your mutual satisfaction and trust that you really care about your mutual happiness.

The communication and negotiating skills that you develop by using the exercises and guidelines of the negotiation tree will overlap into the rest of your activities, such as work and dealing with children, other family members and friends. You will discover that the same techniques that make it easier to work together with your partner also ease all other attempts at communication. When you learn how to present a problem clearly in a way that invites your partner to work on it with you, you will be able to use the same method to address a problem with colleagues. Conflicts resulting from misunderstandings will be rare and, when they do arise, far more easily resolved in all areas of your life.

Over time, this new way of relating as equals who work together can transform your relationship, as it did with Paul and Carol. They realised that Paul needed to learn to take better care of himself, and Carol, who knew how to care for Paul, was learning to be aware of her own needs. As they learned this new, mutually caring attitude through solving simple problems such as who got the car, their way of being together changed. At first, Carol asked for more affection and help with the housework. Paul agreed and asked for help learning what she wanted so he could be warm and caring towards her, and how to take more responsibility around the house.

As they negotiated successfully through a long series of small adjustments over a period of months, they also modified how they behaved towards each other. Paul learned to share his dissatisfaction with his work and to be more affectionate towards Carol, and Carol felt more responsive and generous to Paul as she learned how to have her own needs met. As a result of working together on these and other related issues, Paul was encouraged to get training for a new, more satisfying and better paid job, and Carol became more independent and had more time and energy for her career. They learned to co-operate on household chores, until they became successful enough to employ a cleaner. Their mutual support and lack of conflict at home gave them an extra boost in their careers, both of which thrived as a result.

Couples who know from experience that they can successfully make decisions and feel mutually satisfied and enhanced by being with each other, do not doubt their relationship or their commitment. When a relationship goes well, the reasons for being in it are clear: why would anyone want to leave a relationship where they get what they want all the time? Experience with the negotiation tree will enable you to automatically seek mutually satisfying solutions to every problem that arises and you will be able to build a solid, reliable equal partnership.

THE NEGOTIATION TREE

STEP I: DEFINE AND COMMUNICATE YOUR PROBLEM

IS THE PROBLEM CLEAR TO YOU?

If yes,
state your problem to your partner, get confirmation that it is understood, and proceed to Step II.

If no,
can your partner help you clarify the problem by discussing it?

If yes,
discuss problem until it is defined, then proceed to Step II.

If no,
do it yourself by:

- doing a *problem inventory*, chapter 2, page 28.
- If still unclear, read chapter 2, Define Your Problem, beginning page 18.
- If still unclear, do the *clarifying your wants* exercise, chapter 5, page 109.
- If still unclear, get help from a friend or therapist – see the list of useful addresses on page 151. The umbrella organisations listed will be able to recommend a therapist in your area.

STEP II: AGREE TO NEGOTIATE

DO YOU BOTH AGREE TO NEGOTIATE?

If yes,

proceed to Step III.

If no,

- reassure your partner or ask for reassurance for yourself, as appropriate. Follow the *guidelines for reassurance*, chapter 3, page 61.
- If still no agreement, review chapter 3, Agree to Negotiate, and do the *trouble shooting guide*, chapter 3, page 76.
- If still no agreement, persist using the *guidelines for gentle persistence*, chapter 3, page 74.
- If still no agreement, solve it yourself using the *guidelines for solving it yourself*, chapter 3, page 84.

STEP III: SET THE STAGE (three parts)

A   CHOOSE A TIME AND PLACE: DO YOU BOTH AGREE ON A TIME AND PLACE?

If yes,

proceed to Part B.

If no,

- review steps for *choosing time and place*, chapter 4, page 87.
- If still no agreement, reaffirm your agreement to negotiate (see Step II) and try again using the reassurance and communications skills outlined in chapter 3.

B   ESTABLISH GOODWILL: IS GOODWILL BETWEEN YOU EASILY AVAILABLE?

If yes,

state your goodwill and proceed to Part C.

If no,

- use the *establishing goodwill* guide, chapter 4, page 90.
- If goodwill is not forthcoming, check for held hurt or anger, chapter 4, page 95, and, if necessary, follow the *set aside held hurt and anger guidelines*, chapter 4, page 96.
- If goodwill is still not forthcoming, let a day or two pass and start again.
- If goodwill is still not forthcoming, see a relationship counsellor or psychotherapist.

C   REASSURE: ARE YOU BOTH CONFIDENT OF THE OUTCOME?

If yes,

proceed to Step IV.

If no,

- reassure each other.
- If reassurance isn't working, follow the *guidelines for reassurance*, chapter 4, page 93 and chapter 3, page 61.

STEP IV: STATE YOUR WANTS

ARE YOU EACH CLEAR ABOUT YOUR OWN WANTS?

If yes,

proceed to state your wants.

If no,

- do the exercise on *clarifying your wants*, chapter 5, page 109.
- If still unclear, let a day or two pass and review the *problem inventory*, chapter 2, page 28, then with your problem clearly in your mind, redo the exercise on *clarifying your wants*.

ARE BOTH OF YOU CLEAR ABOUT YOUR PARTNER'S WANTS?

If yes,	If no,
write them out to be certain and proceed to Step V.	<ul><li>follow the *guidelines for sharing wants* in chapter 5, page 116.</li><li>If still unclear, use the *abundance worksheet* in chapter 6, page 125.</li><li>If still unclear and you seem to be stuck, go back to Step III and establish goodwill and reassure. Then try again.</li></ul>

STEP V: EXPLORE YOUR OPTIONS AND DECIDE (four parts)

A   ESTABLISH OPTIONS: ARE VIABLE OPTIONS EASILY AVAILABLE?

If yes,	If no,
choose the option that you can agree upon following the *guidelines for deciding*, chapter 6, page 133, and proceed to Part B.	<ul><li>explore options by expanding boundaries using *the abundance worksheet*, chapter 6, page 125.</li><li>If no option is suitable, do the *brainstorming exercise*, chapter 6, page 122.</li><li>If no option is suitable, explore wants some more using *the abundance worksheet*, chapter 6, page 125.</li><li>If no option is suitable, reassure using the *guidelines for reassurance* if necessary, chapter 4, page 93. Then start with expanding boundaries again (above).</li><li>If you agree on an option and are unsure of its viability, agree to research using the *guidelines for doing research*, chapter 6, page 129.</li><li>If no option is suitable, take a day or two off and come back to it. Review this *negotiation tree* and repeat any parts necessary (e.g. Is this the best time and place to do this? Do we need to re-establish goodwill? Is someone needing reassurance?).</li></ul>

- If no option is suitable, it is possible that the issue being negotiated is a symptom of a deeper problem that can only be resolved with the help of a professional counsellor. It's fine to get professional help, if necessary.

B   CONFIRM YOUR DECISION: DO YOU EACH CLEARLY AGREE TO THE SAME OPTION(S)?

If yes,

follow the *guidelines for confirming your decision* and proceed to Part C.

If no,

- using your communication skills, analyse your concerns and go back to Part A for more exploration.

C   WRITING YOUR AGREEMENT (OPTIONAL)

Follow the *guidelines for finalising your agreement*, chapter 6, page 135, and proceed to Part D.

D   CELEBRATE

Follow the *guidelines for celebration*, chapter 6, page 137.

Although the five steps of co-operative problem solving are simple, we realise there will be many occasions, especially when you are first beginning to learn to use it, when you will get stuck, not know what to do, or fall back into old patterns like competition, arguing, not knowing what you want, misunderstanding each other, or feeling discouraged or confused. At such times you will need help in staying focused on co-operative problem solving or you may find that your negotiation ends in argument and frustration rather than solving the problem. Think of the negotiation tree as a roadmap for problem solving that will guide you, with tested and proven methods, through the problems of problem solving.

HOW TO BEGIN CO-OPERATIVE PROBLEM SOLVING

We strongly recommend reading the book and doing the relevant exercises *before* using the negotiation tree for co-operative problem solving, so that you will have a basic understanding of the terms, guidelines and skills before you use them for the first time. However, if you need to solve something immediately, and cannot wait, you can begin by attempting to solve the problem by following the negotiation tree and allowing it to show you the most appropriate exercises, guidelines, examples and sections of the book for your situation.

When you have read the book, done the exercises and feel ready to try co-operative problem solving, we recommend that you select a problem that seems simple and straightforward. A small problem that doesn't have an emotional charge and seems easy to resolve will give you a chance to learn the process. Try a problem where you normally just let one person make a decision, without negotiation, such as which film to see or where to eat. But this time agree *not* to compromise and negotiate with the intent of both of you getting *exactly* what you want. Because the negotiation tree helps you focus on creative, new ideas, you may find that you will go out dancing or to a play or concert instead of the cinema, or pick up food from two different take-aways so each of you can have different things at the same time!

By keeping the problem simple the first time, you can have a chance to learn how problem solving works. Problems like 'What shall we do this weekend?' or 'Who will do the washing-up tomorrow?' are more likely to be successful first-time experiences than emotionally laden problems like 'We're not having enough sex' that have been long-standing and frustrating to either one or both of you.

Run through the process several times over the next few days, practising with small problems. When you get stuck, use the negotiation tree as your guide to the relevant exercises and instructions. When negotiating small problems becomes easy, challenge yourselves by picking a slightly more difficult problem to negotiate. If you've picked a problem that proves too difficult, either break it down into several, simpler problems (as Suzie and Mike do in the following example) or go to a different, easier problem for more practice and then come back to the more difficult problem again.

When Suzie and Mike negotiate about spending money and find that there is not enough money for both to do what they want to do, they could struggle, argue, or quarrel over who gets what they want. Instead, they realise that they have an opportunity to work together if they break their negotiation down further, from who spends the money to negotiating over how to create more money. As they work together to resolve their money problem, they might discover hidden resources, alternative and inexpensive ways to have what they want. They might find that their lack of money is temporary, a minor inconvenience, and begin to plan to create the extra money they need.

Negotiating is not difficult or painful but, in the beginning, learning a new skill can feel awkward and clumsy. Until you get as familiar with the process as Suzie and Mike are, you may occasionally get stuck or confused while experimenting. This is to be expected and the negotiation tree will tell you what to do if this happens.

As you begin to experiment, you'll see the steps are simple and easy to understand and a little experimentation will convince you that the process works. The only way you can fail is to stop before you learn all the essential skills this book teaches.

With a little practice, you'll find it soon becomes quite comfortable and easy. The aim of co-operation is to make negotiating a pleasant and successful process. In a relatively short time, it can become second nature to negotiate as a partnership; the success rate you will experience when you try this kind of negotiation will be very rewarding.

It is worth taking the extra time to learn this now, because once you become expert, it will make problems easy to solve for the rest of your life and it will give you the confidence to try working together on problems you always thought were impossible to solve. After a few months, you'll be negotiating many aspects of your relationship, until it becomes fully satisfying.

From their experience of co-operative negotiating, equal partners know the effectiveness of working together to solve problems, and the good feeling of teamwork that enhances their goodwill and trust so they face every disagreement, struggle, problem or question with the belief that it can probably be solved in a mutually satisfactory way. They know that the only solution that will really work is a co-operative solution, because a competitive, win/lose solution will undermine their partnership.

This new approach to solving problems works precisely because it is so rewarding. When both of you have enough experience at co-operative problem solving to realise that you can't lose, you will approach disagreements, problems and discussions with a new sense of confidence. You will soon see that each problem-solving session adds new strength and resilience to your relationship, because it adds to your conviction that together you can work anything out successfully.

Once you learn the process, you will consider no problem solved until you both get exactly what you want. You will view each other as partners who enhance and add to each other's ideas and options. The more problems you solve, the stronger your bond becomes.

IF YOUR PARTNER ISN'T CO-OPERATING

*I*deally you and your partner will use the negotiation tree together. Unlike most methods of improving your relationship, however, you can use the negotiation tree to learn better relating and communicating skills and solve relationship problems by yourself. There may be times when you understand co-operative problem solving and are clear about the benefits but your partner is suspicious, uninterested, unavailable or unwilling to try.

The idea of negotiating may sound intimidating to your partner until you both try it and he or she may be hesitant to co-operate at first, but we have provided for that contingency. The negotiation tree shows you exactly how to take the pressure off your partner and yourself and make co-operative negotiation very inviting to you both (see *guidelines for solving it yourself*, page 84).

One of the unique features of the negotiation tree is that it shows you how to be clear about what your problem is, communicate it more effectively to your partner and persist in a way that increases the possibility of enlisting your partner in co-operative negotiation. By reading the book by yourself, even if your partner is uninterested so far, you can still learn co-operative problem solving and how to make co-operation attractive and inviting to a partner. If your partner resists negotiating, the negotiation tree will direct you to the guidelines on *gentle persistence*, which will give you instructions for maximum effectiveness in inviting him or her to co-operate with you.

If you are reading this book on your own, begin by finding a simple problem, defining it so you understand it, and practising how to state the problem clearly. Try co-operative problem solving even though your partner doesn't know about it. Announce to your partner that you need some help with something and then define the problem. Ask if your partner will help you to solve it and negotiate with you. As the negotiation tree says, if you get a yes answer, proceed according to the tree. If you don't, solve the problem for yourself but announce to your partner what your solution is and say that you're still open to negotiation if your partner is interested. This maximises your partner's incentive to join in and work together with you. This will show your partner the benefit of being a part of the solution, even if they know nothing about co-operative problem solving.

IF YOU ARE SINGLE

If you are single and preparing for a future relationship, you can use the negotiation tree to help solve your problem by learning to use co-operative problem solving with friends and family. Knowing how to clearly communicate what is important to you, to accurately understand what a prospective partner wants and needs, and being able to work out differences co-operatively will prepare you for the relationship you want and help you to achieve it smoothly and successfully. When you do find the partner you hope for, having these skills will enable both of you to develop an equal partnership from the beginning.

CHAPTER 2

DEFINE AND COMMUNICATE YOUR PROBLEM

The negotiation tree begins with a seemingly simple instruction: *define the problem*. This first step in negotiation may seem obvious, but its function is to make sure that you understand what the problem is thoroughly enough to clearly communicate that there is a problem in a way your partner can hear and understand. Many couples' problems remain unsolved because, while one partner believes the problem is obvious and self-evident, the other partner is confused or unclear about what's wrong, or is even unaware that there is a problem at all. However, even when both agree there is a problem, they often cannot get the problem clearly defined so that both partners understand it or agree on it, or they don't communicate well (or at all), or they disagree about what the problem is, as in the example of Rose and John, below. You may have have an experience similar to Rose's:

ROSE

Rose is a housewife, in her forties, who feels depressed and unhappy. Rose's whole life for the last twenty-five years has been focused on making her home pleasant and caring for her three children and husband, which was a full-time job. Now, gradually, her major role has become obsolete. The children are young adults and don't need her very much, and her husband, John, a lawyer, is away much of the time in his high-powered career. Rose is unhappy but she has trouble understanding why. She tries to talk to John:

Rose: *John, I don't know what's wrong, but I feel awful.*

John: *Oh, I'm sorry to hear that. Why don't you go to the doctor?*

Rose: *No, it's not that. My health is OK. I just feel listless and tired.*

John: *Are you getting enough rest? Maybe you're still recovering from the flu you had last month.*

Rose: (giving up) *Yes, I suppose you're right.*

John: *Get some extra rest and you'll feel better.* (ends discussion, goes back to the work he brought home)

Rose indeed has a problem, and one that will profoundly affect John if she becomes severely depressed or despondent, but neither of them is clear about what the problem is. John tries, more than some spouses might, to be supportive and caring, but he hasn't enough to go on and has no skills to find out more (and, subconsciously, he may really be afraid to know). He dismisses the problem, Rose gives up, she feels hopeless, and no negotiation takes place. If Rose and John cannot define what the problem is, there is no way they can begin to solve it. The problem is allowed to grow, to become more deep-rooted and to create all kinds of related problems:

- because Rose is depressed, she doesn't do any housework or cooking and John becomes angry; or
- Rose feels so miserable, she is easy prey for an affair, leaving her with massive guilt and even more depression; or
- Rose is so depressed, she doesn't respond sexually, so John is tempted to have an affair; or
- Rose uses alcohol, food or shopping to blunt her pain, and this creates all the havoc that addictions can engender: emotional, physical and/or financial.

In this way, a relatively normal, simple problem, because it was not clearly defined and therefore could not be solved, can become a major catastrophe and even the cause for divorce.

Defining the problem helps the person who is aware that something is wrong. They can then pinpoint and clarify exactly what is upsetting or uncomfortable, which makes it possible to communicate. And communicating it clearly to a partner makes discussion of the problem possible. Surprisingly, couples often find that defining the problem is all they need to do to solve it, because once both people understand what the trouble is, the solution often becomes obvious. For example, if Rose is clear enough about what her problem is to be able to define it to John, things can go very differently:

Rose: (determined to communicate) *John, I feel awful, I think I know why but I need your help and understanding.*

John: *Oh, I'm sorry to hear that – I've got a lot of work to do tonight, but I'll help if I can. What's wrong?*

Rose: (she's thought a lot about it) *I've been very listless and tired lately. I've thought a lot about it, and I think I'm depressed because I don't feel needed anymore.*

John: (not understanding) *Don't be silly, dear, I need you. I wouldn't know what to do without you.*

Rose: (not deterred) *Yes, I know you do, but that's not enough to use all my time and energy. My life has changed since the children have grown up, and it's changed much more than yours has. I need to discuss with you what I can do about it. If I don't do something soon, the way I feel could cause major problems for both of us.*

John: (realising, for the first time, that it's important) *This sounds serious, and I do want to talk to you about it, but I have a lot of work tonight. Can we talk about it later?*

Rose: (making a mental note to bring up the subject at the weekend) *Yes. Now that I know you understand how I feel, I can wait until this weekend to talk.* (Rose knows they can get to the next step, so she ends the discussion, and John goes back to the work he brought home. They'll continue the negotiation process later.)

Because Rose has taken the time to get clear about what her problem is, she is much better able to communicate it to John. She also knows, since she's the one who feels that there is a problem, that it's her responsibility to follow up and make sure she and John work together on it. She is determined not to allow him to ignore the severity of the problem or to put her off and she is prepared to help him understand that, unsolved, this will create problems for him, too. So this step of defining your problem, consists of both the mental exercise of getting clear about what the problem is for you, usually the most difficult part, and a communication exercise, in showing your partner three things:

- that there *is* a problem, whether or not your partner is aware of it;
- what the problem is, in your opinion; and
- the importance of solving the problem (in other words, how your partner will benefit from co-operatively solving this problem, even though he or she has been unaware of it until now).

BARRIERS TO DEFINING YOUR PROBLEM

Although some problems may be easily defined and communicated (you're angry because your partner isn't doing any housework, you don't like the way your partner ignores you at parties, you have a financial problem to discuss), you may encounter more difficulty when you attempt to define problems that are more complex or confusing (you have a vague, pervasive unhappiness, you feel neglected or unappreciated, you're not sure how much responsibility each of you should have). This chapter will help you with those times when you have trouble defining exactly what you need to discuss with your partner. For most people, four common barriers arise when they attempt to define the problem: *confusion, rebellion and compliance, shoulds,* and *secret expectations.*

CONFUSION

Most of us first become aware of a problem because of a vague sense of uneasiness, discomfort, frustration or malaise. Few of us know, instantly and certainly, exactly what is bothering us or what to do about it. You may find yourself thinking, 'If it weren't for (your partner, your job, the weather, etc.) I'd feel better', or even wondering if you're slightly ill ('Maybe I'm coming down with something', 'I've been working too hard', 'It must be the time of the month', 'Perhaps I'm tired').

Sorting through this confusion, learning to be responsive to the inner prompting that says a problem exists rather than ignoring it, and taking enough time to achieve clarity about what's bothering you will make a tremendous difference in your problem-solving abilities. Too often, couples create problems on top of problems by being unclear about what the original difficulty is or by ignoring discomfort or dissatisfaction until the problem has intensified and grown into overwhelming proportions. The exercise later in this chapter (page 25), in the section on confusion, will teach you how to identify, define, and be appropriately aware of potential problems before lack of clarity turns your molehill-sized, everyday problems into mountains.

COMPETITION, REBELLION AND COMPLIANCE

Because the society we live in values competition, and because many people are afraid of losing, and because many of us have been taught to believe that it is self-centred or impolite to say what we want, it can be difficult to tell someone we care about that there is a problem, or that our wants are not being satisfied. On the other hand, if you are successful in business and used to controlling negotiations, it may be difficult to listen while your partner defines a problem. You may automatically jump to the defence, which is a way to win in competition. Approaching problems with a belief that someone wins and someone loses, or that one person is more deserving or powerful than the other, means if you 'lose' you don't get what you want unless you rebel by breaking the agreement, procrastinating or sabotaging. If you choose to rebel, you will feel disruptive, uncooperative, and angry – and the relationship will be in turmoil, with fighting and arguing. Your other option, as the one who 'lost', is to comply. If you comply, you will feel powerless, depressed and, eventually, enraged. Your relationship will seem smooth for a while, but after giving in for a while, your anger will seep out in subtle, passive/aggressive ways, perhaps losing sexual desire, being depressed and miserable, falling ill or in periodic explosions over insignificant issues.

If Rose accepted that all problems result in someone winning and the other person losing, she might have assumed that John would 'win' and everything would have to stay as it was. Then she might not have brought the problem up until she was so upset, depressed or desperate that she had to. Or, she might have decided that to 'win' she would have to rebel, get angry and make demands of John, who would then probably react to her attitude and struggle against her. In the first example, Rose did bring the problem up, but gave up easily and complied with what she thought he wanted, feeling she had 'lost'.

Neither compliance nor rebellion leads to mutually satisfactory solutions, because one partner always gets less while the other gets more, which leads to guilt, disappointment, frustration and anger. The exercises in the compliance and rebellion section will teach you how to avoid either extreme and instead negotiate as equals, with equal votes and veto power, so neither of you feels you have to give up what you want (comply) or declare domestic war (rebel).

SHOULDS

All of us have rules that define who we are, and how we live – things we feel we should or should not do, such as the Ten Commandments, rules of etiquette, and standards that define behaviour as generous or selfish. Some of these rules are well-reasoned ideas we have developed out of our life experience, and that work well for us, and others are unconscious prejudices and mistaken beliefs we acquired by early training and observation of flawed role models, which we have never had cause to examine or change.

We all grow up with ideas of how we should be in relationships, what the proper roles for persons of our gender are, and how husbands, wives and single people must act. No matter why we have these internal *shoulds*, if they are too rigid, they can become limiting or problematic, interfering with our happiness and success in life and in our relationships. Believing you should do something or behave a certain way can be a barrier to defining and communicating your problem, because when your needs, desires or the reality of your situation challenges or contradicts a *should*, you will feel confusion and guilt as a result. To avoid this discomfort you will suppress or ignore what you really want, and without that knowledge you cannot create a truly satisfying life for yourself.

In the section about shoulds, you will learn about cultural rules and family rules for being who you are, exercises to make these rules more adaptable to your actual life by turning your shoulds into permissions. These exercises will help you explore the unconscious rules that may be running your relationship and help you to achieve the freedom of choice you need to create a co-operative and mutually satisfying partnership.

SECRET EXPECTATIONS

It is often considerate, gracious or polite to try to guess what the people around you want and need from you. You may have developed the ability so well that you are often accurate. However, in an intimate relationship, when you make guesses about what your partner wants and needs, and your partner in return makes guesses about you, it is very easy to interpret each other's signals differently. As a result, you and your partner can believe you have a clear understanding without realising that your interpretation of the agreement is different.

Sooner or later, your expectations will not be fulfilled, because your partner guessed wrong about what they are, and hurt feelings, upsets and even rage can result. When you feel very confused or more upset than the problem warrants, you and your partner have probably developed a *secret expectation*, or an unconscious set of 'shoulds', that can be one of the major reasons why problems between couples do not get solved. The exercises that accompany the negotiation tree will help you understand what secret expectations are, how they develop and what to do about them. When your secret expectations are no longer secret, the source of many mysterious and confusing upsets in your relationship will be astoundingly clear. Once a secret expectation is exposed and understood, it will no longer trouble you.

For example, Don and Peter, a committed gay couple, may think they have a clear agreement about housework. Don thinks his job is taking out the rubbish and Peter washes the dishes. Peter may think he is supposed to wash the dishes, while Don waters the plants. Although most of the time everything gets done, for a couple of weeks Don doesn't water the plants, assuming Peter will do it. When the plants begin to wilt, Peter accuses Don of not doing his share around the house. Don, who has been faithfully taking out the rubbish, even though he was busy, is highly insulted and feels unjustly accused.

They have just experienced the result of an unclear, covert, assumed understanding   a secret expectation. Secret expectations can obviously create difficulty and interfere with defining your problem because they create confusion, which makes communication difficult.

A secret expectation exists when you make guesses about what your partner wants and force your partner to guess, by not being open about what you want. Secret expectations are 'secret' because no one ever states out loud, 'I want you to . . .' or asks, 'What do you want?' or 'Would you like me to . . . ?' In short, no one clearly defines the problem. Secret or covert expectations are common in relationships, because the partners try to read each other's mind and please a partner by anticipating what he or she wants.

The exercises in the secret expectations section of this chapter will teach you how to tell when secret expectations are operating and how to bring them into the open, so you can clearly define your problem or communicate effectively with your partner. You will learn how to renegotiate them into clear, effective, open agreements.

The exercises in the defining the problem section will teach you the skills to overcome all four of these barriers – *confusion, rebellion and compliance, shoulds,* and *secret expectations.* We have provided you with information to draw up a:

- *problem inventory* to help you define and communicate your needs and wants clearly, so both you and your partner can understand the problem and learn to translate your negative statements (what you don't want) into positive statements (what you do want), which overcomes the barrier of confusion;

- *compliance and rebellion inventory* to help you recognise and disarm competition, compliance, or rebellion when it arises;
- *method of creating permission*, which will teach you how to disarm shoulds; and
- *rights and responsibilities analysis*, which will help you change your secret expectations into open agreements.

With these skills, you will be able to successfully define and communicate your problem and move on to the next step, the *agreement to negotiate*.

CONFUSION

Often when we know we're unhappy or that something is wrong, it is difficult to get a clear enough idea of exactly what is wrong to convey it to someone else. In our experience, many people who come for counselling know they're unhappy and that their relationship doesn't seem to be working, but are confused because they do not understand why. So, the first step towards helping find a solution is helping them sort through their confusion and define and communicate their problem.

That means you need to learn about *how* to communicate problems to your partner in such a way that he or she can hear and understand, yet not feel defensive or hopeless about solving them. Good communication will make it more likely that you will have your partner's help in solving the problem and, therefore, that the difficulty will get satisfactorily solved.

Defining the problem includes explaining to your partner why solving the problem is beneficial to both of you, because, until your partner understands the gains to be derived from solving it, it won't seem worth the effort and the problem will seem to be only yours. The better you are at defining it and making it clear why and how your problem will impact on your partner, the more motivated your partner will be to help you solve it.

If you recognise that a problem exists but you feel vague or confused about exactly what it is, the following *problem inventory* will help you sort through confusion and understand the problem clearly. By taking the time to list and evaluate the *indicators* and create a clear statement of the problem, you can greatly enhance the effectiveness of your communication with your partner, because you'll understand the problem enough to explain it. A clear explanation will motivate your partner to want to solve the problem because the benefit will be understood, and you'll be able to work together co-operatively to solve the problems faster and easier before they become a source of trouble.

EXERCISE

....

THE PROBLEM INVENTORY

To do this exercise, you'll need a pencil or pen and paper, some quiet, undisturbed time and a comfortable place to be alone, to think and to write. The first time you use the negotiation tree, choosing a simple problem to solve will make this problem inventory (and also defining the problem) easier. But, no matter how difficult or long-standing your problem is, the problem inventory, by showing you how to analyse the indicators that a problem exists, will help you better understand why it is a problem for you, so you can communicate it more clearly to your partner.

1 LIST THE PROBLEM INDICATORS

No matter how confused or uncertain you may be over what your problem is, you do know it's there. That means there is some feeling (sadness, anger, confusion), physical sensation (tightness in the chest, a tension headache), circumstance (one of you is putting off doing chores or paying the bills), or interaction with your partner (one of you was critical or angry for no apparent reason) that has made you aware that there *is* a problem. These are your *problem indicators*.

Confusion is usually caused by a number of conflicting or competing ideas and feelings that are all trying to get your attention at once. By listing the problem indicators, you can see each one individually, and your confusion will lessen. On your paper, make a heading 'Problem Indicators' and write down whatever experience or feeling it was that first indicated to you that there might be a problem. For example, Rose's list might read:

- I'm crying a lot;
- I feel frustrated;
- I feel useless;
- there's not enough to do;
- I'm eating too much;
- I'm fantasising about having another baby;
- John seems to be pushing me away.

List everything that seems to indicate you have a problem, even if it seems too obvious to mention, such as a quarrel between you and your partner, or too silly, such as a dream or a passing thought that seems connected.

The more complex or long-standing your problem is, the more time you will have had to develop and observe indicators, so the longer your list will be. Taking the time to think about why and how you know there's a problem will also help you to become aware of the less obvious indicators, too, because you'll stop ignoring or glossing over them when you give them some thought. Don't rush this step: take enough time, at least ten to fifteen minutes.

If you feel very confused about a particular problem, you may need to take longer on this step, putting your list down for a few minutes, an hour, or even a day or two, and adding to it as new insights occur to you. When you finally think your list includes all the important indicators, go to Step 2.

2 EVALUATE YOUR INDICATORS

Review each indicator on your list. Look for central themes of emotion, things or situations: are your indicators about time, money, power or control, freedom, loss, comfort, sadness, anger, fear, self-criticism, frustration?

If there are several items about crying, depression or loss, that would indicate a theme of sadness. If several items are about being rushed, no time to play or wasting time, that's a time theme. Identifying a theme of emotion, things or situations gives you a way to evaluate and understand the hidden meaning of your indicators and organise them into categories, which will make the more subtle dynamics of the problem clearer.

Next to each indicator on your list, write the appropriate theme. If you're not sure what the theme for one indicator is, put a question mark next to it and go on to the others. After you get through the rest of the themes, the one you were unsure of may be clearer, and you can write the theme next to the question mark. If not, go back to Step 1 and think about it a little more and see if you can find more indicators that will make the theme come clear. If it's not clear, put it aside until after you've done Step 3, and concentrate on the items you do feel clear about.

Here's what Rose's list looked like after this step:

- I'm crying a lot (loss);
- I feel frustrated (?) [on second attempt] (time, loss, self-criticism);
- I fell useless (self-criticism);
- there's not enough to do (time);
- I'm eating too much (self-criticism, comfort);
- fantasising about having a another baby (loss);
- John seems to be pushing me away (loss).

Rose's list is about time (too much on her hands), loss (children are not around much anymore, John ignoring her) and self-criticism (she feels useless, eats too much to comfort herself).

3 PUT THE THEMES INTO A SENTENCE

Now, below your indicator list, write the themes you found. Rose's list would be 'time, loss, self-criticism'. Using these themes, compose a sentence or two that describes the problem. Rose wrote: 'I'm experiencing loss, because my children have left home and I have time on my hands. Now that I'm not taking care of them and John anymore, I criticise myself a lot and I feel worthless'.

Because Rose's problem was important and complex, she didn't come up with that sentence immediately. She had to think about her themes for a while first, and she wrote several descriptions before she found the one that fitted.

If your problem is simple and your confusion is mild (you're annoyed about feeding the dog and a little confused about whose job it should be), listing the indicators and themes may make the problem clear to you very easily. If the problem is more deeply rooted or long-standing, and you have a lot of confusion, like Rose, you will have to think about the themes for a while before you can relate them to each other and express your problem in sentence form. When you have completed your sentence, go on to the next step.

If you have a lot of trouble identifying themes and creating a sentence, put this exercise aside and do the exercises that follow in this chapter. As you explore your own relationship to rebellion and compliance, shoulds and secret expectations, you'll discover what blocks prevent you from clarifying the problem. Then return to finish this exercise.

Note: Once in a while, during this exercise, someone will realise that the confusion is a result of some deep inner problem, such as early childhood trauma, an addiction, or severe emotional upset, that is too complex to be solved without professional help. In that case, take your problem indicator list with the themes to a counsellor or psychotherapist for guidance.

4 REVIEW FOR CLARITY

Now that you have clarified your confusion and have a description of the problem that you understand, the next step is to make sure it will be clear and not confusing to your partner.

Review your descriptive sentence from Step Three as though you were reading it for the first time, to see whether it's clear enough to be understandable to your partner.

You may want to say it out loud, or tape-record it, to get the full impact of how it sounds.

If you like, you can pretend your partner is sitting opposite you and you can practise explaining the problem to him or her. Your purpose is simply to define the problem and not to express your feelings. If you let frustration or resentment creep in and phrase the problem in terms of blaming someone (even yourself), your partner will probably react with defensiveness and confusion, and you won't be able to move ahead in your negotiation.

Keep in mind that you're describing the problem as you experience it. State in terms of yourself: for example, Rose will be more likely to be heard if she says, 'I feel useless and not very important now that the children have grown up', than if she says, 'The children never telephone, and you're neglecting me'. John can be more sympathetic and less defensive if he doesn't feel criticised or attacked. (If you now clearly understand what your problem is, but you cannot express it without resentment or fear, read the next section on compliance and rebellion.)

Review and refine your statement of the problem until you are ready to communicate it positively to your partner and you feel quite sure your partner will be able to understand it.

5 LEARN FROM YOUR EXPERIENCE

This final step of this exercise will help you become more sensitive to the signals that tell you a problem exists, which will make recognising and defining your problem easier as time goes on. Review what you've learned about your confusion while you were doing the previous steps of this exercise, to analyse what your indicators are. For example, a tense feeling in the pit of your stomach, a headache, exhaustion or depression might be an indicator that shows up whenever you have a problem, and by becoming sensitive to these recurring signs, you can become aware of unsolved problems much sooner.

As you do this exercise several times for different problems, you will begin to see a pattern to the indicators. For example, Rose often eats too much when she is unhappy but has not yet defined the problem. By becoming aware of this indicator, whenever she notices she's overeating, she can immediately take the time to define her problem, stop the overeating and handle the problem while it's still small and manageable. Your recurring indicators may include butterflies in your stomach, sleep disturbances or dreams, or irritability. Once you know these are just problem indicators they will not be as upsetting, and they will subside. When you've done this exercise many times, it will become quite easy to analyse your problem indicators and define the problem quickly, without formally writing them down.

COMPLIANCE AND REBELLION

*E*ven after you have done the problem inventory and you feel clear about what your problem is, you may find you are still reluctant to approach your partner with the problem, or you may still have some difficulty articulating it calmly. If you feel like attacking or blaming your partner or fighting about the issue, or you're reluctant or afraid to bring the problem to your partner, you are probably experiencing either rebellion or compliance. It is another aspect of the win/lose competitive attitude we have discussed before. In this case, the struggle is about who has the power, or is dominant, in the relationship.

Rebellion is defying someone because you feel he or she is trying to manipulate or control you. Compliance is giving in or trying to placate and please someone whom you feel has the right or power to control you. Both feelings are based on the belief that the power between you is unequal because one person has, or seems to have, more power than the other. Co-operative negotiation cannot take place between unequal partners, because if you are the partner who feels powerless, you either will comply and not say clearly what is wrong or rebel by blaming and accusing your partner instead of communicating your problem.

Traditional relationship styles have often promoted unequal power, leading people to believe that one partner should dominate while the other complies. Hence many couples assume their relationship has room for only one person in charge. But operating this way leaves one partner feeling like a parent (responsible and in charge) and the other feeling like a child (irresponsible or abused). Neither partner feels satisfied, respected, loved for who they are, or equal. While it is appropriate as well-rounded adults in a healthy relationship to do parental or childlike things occasionally (you can comfort each other, either of you may take the most responsibility for a particular chore or situation, you can both be playful and silly when you're having fun), if you feel you have no choice but to play one of those roles (feeling stuck with too much responsibility or not enough power), you will respond with rebellion or compliance, which produces friction, tension and confusion. Consequently, both you and your partner will feel dissatisfied, frustrated, unequal, resentful and unhappy.

As a normal, intelligent adult, you have the capacity to be equal. If you have not been equal in your relationship, it is because your inner inequality has created the outer inequality. Learning to interact as equal partners means you will begin by acting as if you are equal, and in the process, actually become equal partners, carrying your share of the relationship responsibilities and no more.

Although you may not realise it, many of the restrictions that you rebel against or comply with are self-imposed and have little to do with your partner's attempting to control or coerce you. It is even possible to interpret your partner's behaviour to be controlling when it is not intended to be. For example, if your partner says, 'I'd like to get up early', you can interpret that to mean, 'We have to get up early or I'll be angry', without ever questioning it. You may feel that you should do certain things in certain ways because it's the right thing to do or everybody does it that way. If you were strictly brought up, you may now be controlling yourself as rigidly as your family once did and thinking the control comes from your partner.

Your partner may not be trying to control you but by giving in without objecting, you make it seem that way. Even if he or she does tend to tell you what to do, it may or may not be intentional, just a habit carried over from the workplace or from past experience. If your wife supervises a number of people at work, she may continue behaving at home as she does all day towards her subordinates, giving orders and organising them. If your husband has had a previous relationship with a passive woman, he may be used to deciding everything and forget you're more independent.

Compliance and rebellion often exist, not because your partner is trying to control you, but because you are expecting yourself to do things in certain rigid ways (or not allowing yourself to relax until stringent – perhaps impossible – requirements are met).

For most people, the unequal interaction that prompts rebellion or compliance is merely based on confusion and old habit patterns, and is quite easily solved by learning co-operative negotiation, which teaches you to solve problems like the equal, competent adult that you are. However, if you have a history of being in unsuccessful relationships or are a survivor of childhood abuse, this issue of compliance or rebellion will be a very big one for you. You might want to seek counselling to help you learn to protect yourself and maintain your equality.

EXERCISE

COMPLIANCE AND REBELLION INVENTORY

In the following exercise you will learn to recognise when you are acting out of rebellion or compliance, how to discuss your interaction with your partner and consider and decide what changes you wish to make in your interaction to make it more equal.

If you and your partner are working on this book together, each of you can do this exercise separately. To avoid being confused or having your answers influenced or distorted by each other, do not share or discuss your answers until you are instructed to do so.

Fill in the blanks in the statements below with 'always', 'usually', 'sometimes', 'seldom' or 'never'.

1 When something needs to be done around the house, I _____ initiate the necessary action.
2 I am _____ in charge of how we spend money.
3 I _____ feel angry when I am left out of decisions.
4 I _____ find it harder to do something if my partner wants me to.
5 I will _____ fight to win an argument even if I know I'm wrong.
6 I _____ feel like a parent, the boss, or otherwise in charge.
7 My partner _____ feels like an extra burden or responsibility for me.
8 I _____ resist asking for help or being taken care of.
9 I am _____ sure that my partner can't manage things as well as I can.
10 When the household chores need doing, I _____ double-check to see if my partner is doing what he or she is supposed to.

Rate your answers as follows: 1 point for each 'always' or 'usually', 2 for each 'sometimes', and 3 for each ' seldom' or 'never'. Now add up your score and compare it to the following analysis:

10–15 points – You won't have a difficult time defining your problem or understanding what it is, because you are used to being in charge, knowing what's wrong and what to do about it. The problem may be that you will also try to define everyone else's problem for them. You may also have trouble communicating a problem to your partner or getting his or her co-operation, because you have a tendency to tell your partner what the solution should be (which causes your partner to rebel and argue, or comply and insincerely agree, clam up, or not participate) rather than negotiating and creating the solution with your partner. In the following discussion, make an extra effort to listen to your partner's feelings, ideas and opinions, rather than focusing on your own ideas and solutions.

16–25 points – You feel quite equal to your partner, are more willing to negotiate and are probably pretty evenly balanced between being compliant and rebellious. You value teamwork and mutual agreement. Defining your problem is fairly easy for you, because you are used to thinking for yourself and you will probably be able to communicate it well enough for your partner to understand. You will probably enjoy the ensuing discussion and it will help you build even more teamwork, because you will keep an even balance between listening to your partner and sharing your own thoughts.

26–30 points – Even when you have used the problem inventory to help you, you will probably have some trouble defining your problem, because you will have trouble feeling your needs are important enough to bring the problem up with your partner. But, if you allow the problem to go un-negotiated, you will eventually resent the situation and feel unsatisfied and trapped. In the discussion section that follows, concentrate on speaking up for yourself and invite your partner to help you be more assertive about what you want. If this seems impossible, get some professional help, perhaps from Relate.

THE DISCUSSION:

With your partner or a good friend, discuss the way you completed the statements on page 30 as follows:

1 COMPARE ANSWERS

Re-read each of the completed sentences, compare your answers and each of you take two minutes or less to explain why you answered 'always', 'usually', 'sometimes', 'seldom' or 'never' to that particular statement. This will help you better understand the ways you rebel or comply and your reasons, which will help you be aware of and correct the behaviour as you learn to problem solve as equals.

2 COMPARE SCORES

Compare your total scores, read the appropriate score interpretation paragraphs and discuss whether you think the evaluation is appropriate for yourself and your partner. If your opinion of your own attitudes of compliance and rebellion differs from what the interpretation says, say why you think it's different. If your opinion is that the evaluation is accurate, say why. Now do the same for each other's evaluation. This will also help you understand and be more aware of rebelling and complying. Then you can begin to interact more as an equal with your partner to improve your communication and problem solving.

3 CONSIDER CHANGES

Discuss how your power roles (feeling like a parent or child) and patterns of compliance (giving in to or placating your partner) and rebellion (blaming, arguing or fighting back) hinder your problem solving and communication, and how it prevents you from communicating it to your partner. Talk about how you have fought back, complied or given up in other situations and previous relationships, including your childhood. Also discuss situations in which you have discussed a problem as an equally powerful person and how that helped you work together. Finish the discussion by recapping how your compliant or rebellious attitudes have created problems in the past and how you can change your behaviour (by saying what you want, not agreeing when you don't want to, calmly giving your different opinion instead of blaming or fighting) so you can solve problems more as equals in the future.

Now that you have tallied your scores, and reviewed or discussed your answers, you have a clearer idea of how much you comply or rebel in your relationship. You may be quite surprised to find out how restricted you feel and that both you and your partner feel restricted in similar or different ways. Knowing how these restrictions have hindered your problem solving in the past can motivate you to change your old habits of rebellion or compliance and strive to become more equal partners by learning co-operative negotiation.

SHOULDS: RULES, CUSTOMS AND TRADITIONS

If you are feeling unhappy, uncomfortable or frustrated in some aspect of your relationship and you are having trouble defining your problem, you may be in conflict with, or unaware of, your own internal rules for relationship and how relationship rules work. For example, if Rose believes she 'should' be happy and fulfilled as a housewife, she'll have trouble admitting or understanding that she is unhappy because her life lacks meaning.

Your observations of the society you live in, the patterns and traditions in your family when you were growing up and what you were told as you grew up, combine to form a largely unconscious list of 'rules' for being in relationships. Because we learn the rules for living in our family as small children, without the ability to judge or evaluate what we are taught, we are never able to examine these rules for effectiveness, functionality and health before they are imposed on us. These rules are seldom learned directly but by inference, example, and often painful experience. That is, seldom does anyone tell you how you must be in your relationship, but through approval and disapproval of you and others and through example, your family, friends and partners teach you what is expected of you. Because you learned them as a naive child who believed what you were told, these rules appear to be facts, written in stone. But often they're mistaken or wrong or even destructive.

There are several kinds of 'shoulds' that can be operating in your life and your relationship. Traditional rules are the social customs that you acquired by observing others and through childhood experience. They often seem like hard facts but you'll find that when you look at them closely, many of them seem less logical. Many of these traditional rules are changing in today's society, but most of us are old enough to have learned them as correct attitudes and behaviour, even if we don't agree with them. You can tell when these 'shoulds' are operating because you will use words like 'acceptable', 'right', 'proper', and 'normal' when you think about them. You see society's rules in the street, on television and in films and when you're at gatherings of people – at a party, in the pub or at work. They are the unspoken rules most people seem to follow and the ones that people are laughed at or looked down upon for not following. Examples of traditional rules are:

- men open doors for women and allow them to go first;
- women wait to be asked;
- don't talk openly and honestly about emotions, sex or money;
- lying or denying is better than upsetting people.

Gender stereotypes are a form of 'shoulds' that define our roles as men and women in our culture, often according to our ethnic heritage. Even though these roles are changing today, many of us were brought up to believe that men should behave in one way and women in another and these ways may not be compatible with who the individual men and women are. The 'rules' for your own gender affect your behaviour and those for the other gender affect your choice of a partner, or, if you are in a same-sex relationship, they may affect the roles you play. Some examples of gender stereotypes are:

- men shouldn't be too emotional;
- women don't handle money well;
- a single man avoids commitment, a single women wants marriage;
- a man is responsible in the world, a woman is responsible in the home.

In addition to all these unwritten rules for behaviour within society, your family had its own expectations. These are messages you received in childhood about how men and women should behave: 'a lady doesn't sit like that', 'big boys don't cry', 'the man controls the money in the relationship', 'the father supports the family', or 'the wife has to make her husband happy'. Also, there are family rules you learned from watching what adults did:

- Daddy (therefore all men) shouts when there's a problem, but Mummy (therefore all women) suffers silently;
- it's grown-up and sexy to smoke (drink, drive fast);
- problems are never talked about, there's just a lot of tension in the air;
- the family is more important than the individual in it.

If Rose was brought up to believe that women are supposed to be fully satisfied within the home and are not supposed to make waves, she could have a lot of trouble even realising why she was unhappy and even more difficulty in explaining the situation so that John could understand. As long as Rose was content at home, the rule was no problem, but, when circumstances changed, Rose was trapped by her compliance with a rule that no longer applied.

Because you and your partner grew up in different families, with their own ways of doing things, and because you had different experiences in life, each of you will have beliefs about how you should be in relationships, and whenever you encounter a situation where your differing rules collide, conflict is almost guaranteed. Each of you will feel very strongly that the other is not doing what should be done.

If Paul's mother had been home with him all the time when he was a child and Carol's mother worked, Paul and Carol will most likely have conflicting ideas – built on their different childhood experiences – about the woman's role in the relationship. While Paul and Carol might both enjoy (or need) the money Carol's career generates, when she can't get home from work before Paul she may be shocked and confused by how unreasonably resentful or angry he is.

Like Carol and Paul, most of us are unaware of the 'shoulds' that describe how we are supposed to be in a relationship. Social rules can be useful and without some mutually understood guidelines for proper behaviour, we would not be able to create an orderly society. But they often cause problems in intimate relationships. Pre-ordained guidelines for social and business behaviour and interaction, such as correct ways to meet new people, good manners and proper business behaviour, help bring order to our lives and guide us in dealing comfortably with strangers, business associates and social contacts. But in close relationships, we go far beyond the kinds of interactions (how to address strangers, how to behave at a party, how to conduct a meeting) these social rules address: we become intimate, which means we get to know each other's more private selves and we interact on an emotional level, not a social one. To make intimacy work, we must deal with each other as caring individuals. If attempting to guide sexual partnerships by 'shoulds' worked well, relationships wouldn't be so difficult and fail so often, and marital and child abuse would have been eliminated generations ago.

Becoming aware of your traditional, social and family rules makes it possible for you to clearly understand the difference between what you 'should' do and what will be effective and satisfying. Understanding that 'shoulds' are not necessarily functional and may be in conflict with what you actually need to be happy and fulfilled, can help you whenever you feel locked in a struggle, confused or unable to solve a problem.

For example, Carol believes that, as a woman, she must take care of Paul and his needs before she takes care of herself, so she has trouble realising that she is overburdened and her depression and anxiety are a result of her stress. Paul, too, believes that, as a man, he shouldn't be concerned about his emotional needs or his own comfort. As long as they do not examine these beliefs, they will feel frustrated, unhappy and trapped in roles that aren't working and keep their relationship from being satisfying. The danger of having unconscious rules is that you will either comply with or rebel against these 'shoulds' and never really get to know how *you* want to do it.

'Shoulds' can prevent you from defining your problem by:

- making you believe you shouldn't have the problem. (Rose may be intelligent but her 'shoulds' say she should be a housewife, so she can't have a problem related to wanting more.)

- being inappropriate to our lives as adults. (As a child, Paul learned not to complain or speak up when he was unhappy, but now it prevents him from letting Carol know what problems they could solve in the relationship.)
- causing you to believe you can't accept what is obviously a good solution. (Carol and Paul need the extra money, but Paul's belief that women stay at home makes him resist Carol's working, even though she wants to.)
- requiring you to deny some of your natural abilities and aspirations. (John would like to take guitar lessons but his 'shoulds' say that's too frivolous, so he says he's too busy with work.)
- making it impossible for you to communicate, because you have different 'shoulds' about how to do it. (Peter learned that whoever shouted loudest won the argument, Don learned not to talk about it at all, so Peter shouts, Don clams up and they never define the problem.)

Understanding that these subconscious rules exist will make it much easier for you to understand why you feel confused, unable or reluctant to define your problem. Whenever you feel stuck, you can search for the 'should' or the rule that is restricting you and in its place create permission. This will make it easier to define a problem by giving you the freedom to act according to what is actually needed, rather than be limited by rules that may not apply.

Go back to the first exercise, the problem inventory, and reread your indicator list. You may discover that many cultural, family, traditional and personal rules have added to your confusion and prevented you from seeing the problem clearly before.

Even when both partners agree on some 'shoulds', rigid adherence to specific rules doesn't work in the long run because it is boring and tiring, and circumstances (such as illness, change of job or business travel) may make it necessary to change behaviour from time to time. Having permission to change your relationship in whatever way works is much more realistic and sustainable. Creating permission gives you the flexibility to be able to make your rules more flexible when they conflict, communicate more openly and honestly about what's wrong, and therefore, to define problems readily.

CREATING PERMISSION

Once you realise how traditional, gender and family rules for behaviour have been preventing you from defining your problem and you know what some of these rules are, the next step is to give yourself permission to change 'shoulds' into 'coulds'.

The easiest way past the barrier of 'shoulds' is to think 'I could', instead. That is, you can create permission to either follow, alter or ignore the rule. In this way, you can take each rule that causes problems in your relationship and change it into a permission or a choice.

For example, one of Rose's rules was: 'Women are supposed to be fully satisfied within the home'. She rewrote that rule as permissions as follows: 'As a woman, I *could* choose to work or be a housewife, depending on what I want and what my needs are'. Following that example, rewrite each of the traditional rules, gender stereotypes and family rules listed as examples on page 33.

When 'shoulds' are combined with uncommunicated expectations, they create confusion and chaos. This makes it very difficult to think clearly enough to define, understand and communicate the problem – the dynamic of *secret expectations*.

SECRET EXPECTATIONS

Secret expectations form quite easily, because most of us make assumptions about the future from what has happened before. If Iris and Jan meet on a Wednesday and then the next week Jan phones and asks Iris out on Wednesday night and the following week it happens again, when the fourth week arrives and Jan doesn't call, what will Iris think? She'll most likely be upset, because she thought they were going out every Wednesday. What Iris doesn't know, because it wasn't mentioned, is that Jan has a late business meeting every fourth Wednesday night; Jan doesn't realise that Iris has a secret expectation that Wednesday is their night out. Iris' expectation that Jan would phone has led her to believe that something is wrong, that Jan may have stopped wanting to see her, because she doesn't know the facts. Iris will be hurt, disappointed and possibly upset, and she and Jan may even have an argument over it.

Secret expectations can get even more emotionally loaded when they are connected to 'shoulds' left over from childhood. If Paul expects Carol to serve dinner at 6:00 every night, because that's what his mother always did, that's a 'should'. If, in addition, he (probably without being aware of it) believes Carol's serving dinner on time means she loves him (and she doesn't care for him if dinner is not ready), then Paul's got a secret expectation. If Carol doesn't know about Paul's expectation and he doesn't realise that Carol doesn't think dinner on time is very important, a relationship problem is brewing and will catch them by surprise. Things can get even more complicated if Paul thinks Carol's supposed to get dinner ready for 6:00 to show she loves him and she thinks she's supposed to iron his shirts to show love. Carol may be working very hard at ironing shirts to let Paul know he's loved and he might be getting angrier and angrier because dinner is late.

Secret expectations can usually be spotted when you or your partner overreact to an event. If Carol doesn't have dinner ready at 6:00 when Paul gets home but leaves a note (on his freshly ironed shirts!) that she's gone to her mother's for dinner and there's a frozen dinner in the freezer, he may be very upset. Instead of asking what happened, Paul overreacts to the surprise, throws a fit and threatens to divorce her. Carol is completely mystified and confused and feels unjustly accused of not loving him, because she can only see that he's overeacting to missing dinner.

Long-standing resentment is another telltale sign of hidden expectations. If you have hidden expectations of how your partner should behave and he or she doesn't comply (because you haven't let your wishes be known), resentment will slowly build up, sometimes until it is released in a rage. In our earlier example, Peter might not say anything when the plants are not watered (partner Don doesn't realise it's his job in Peter's eyes), and go ahead and water them, but if it happens a few times, Peter will get angrier and angrier, until one day he explodes.

Changing your secret expectations into open agreements, as in the last section, disarms them and eleminates the resentment and arguments they cause, while making it much easier to clearly define problems when they come up. Once the secret is out, and you realise expectations exist, it can be quite simple to make an open agreement. The following exercise will help you become aware of your secret expectations, so you can turn them into permission and proceed to negotiate wherever you disagree about your expectations.

EXERCISE

DISCOVERING SECRET EXPECTATIONS

Because the indicators are irritation, frustration, resentment or any reaction that is out of proportion to what really happened (as when Paul blows up because Carol isn't home to cook dinner), by reviewing your relationships for these overreactions, you can backtrack to discover what secret expectations are at work. Carol for example, might look into her past relationships for some clues to her secret expectation.

1 Mentally review your past relationships for trouble spots. Were there times when your partner got extremely angry, hurt, afraid or upset about something you did or didn't do? Write a brief description of what happened: *Paul got unreasonably angry when I wasn't home to cook dinner, even though I ironed his shirts and told him where I was.*

2 Now, review your own behaviour in those relationships. Were there times when *you* got upset, angry, frustrated, or disappointed out of proportion to what your partner did or didn't do? Write a brief description: *I got very angry when Paul didn't appreciate my ironing enough. I fumed about it for days.*

3 Look at these two lists and try to imagine what the expectations were when the overreactions happened: *Paul must have expected that I would always be home to cook dinner and I must have expected that he would appreciate my ironing his shirts enough to not mind getting his own dinner.*

4 Turn your expectations into permission, by putting 'could' or 'can' in place of 'should'. *I can let Paul know I love him in other ways than by making dinner and ironing shirts. We can talk about what our responsibilities are in the relationship.*

If possible, using the above information, discuss your secret expectations with your partner and seek to discover when they exist by becoming aware of resentment and overreactions as they happen. Talk about the warning signs you see in yourself and in your partner, the kinds of secret expectations you have had in the past and what you can do to correct them. When you detect one, turn the expectation into permission and work out a solution together, using problem solving if necessary. Discuss how to bring up the subject in a way that can be heard when either of you believes that your partner is harbouring a secret expectation. They often arise when partners don't openly discuss the rights and responsibilities each one has in the relationship. Acknowledging these rights and responsibilities and agreeing on them makes defining your problem easier because it helps eliminate secret expectations and the resulting confusion.

RIGHTS AND RESPONSIBILITIES

As partners, you have rights in your relationship (just as you do in our society) and along with these rights come certain responsibilities. For example, partners have a right to have reasonable sexual needs met and a responsibility to keep a positive emotional atmosphere that's conducive to lovemaking. You also have a right to be clearly communicated with (and listened to) and a responsibility to do your share of the communicating (and listening). But when partners have different ideas about each partner's rights and responsibilities, it can be a barrier to defining your problem. If you do not feel you have the right to ask for what you want or to be satisfied, you will not be able to communicate your dissatisfaction to your partner. Couples often make the mistake of assuming they know (without stating aloud) what their individual rights and responsibilities are, which leads to having secret, rather than open, agreements. Learning to be aware of, and communicate, your mutual rights and responsibilities helps you create open agreements and clearly define any problems that arise.

As an equal partner, you have a responsibility to assume an equal share of the normal financial, practical and social obligations of life. That doesn't mean you have to keep the score and always contribute equally, but your agreement must feel mutual. In addition, you have a responsibility to keep your relationship sustainable, that is, to take care of yourself, to ask for help when you need it (but have other options in case the answer is no) and to co-operate with your partner as much as you can without resenting, being deprived or feeling damaged by what's requested of you.

Equal partners rights' include:

- being able to ask for what you want (and find another solution if the answer is no);
- saying no to your partner, in order to take care of yourself;
- doing what you need to do to be happy, healthy and satisfied;
- co-operating with your partner in order to create a relationship that you enjoy.

The following exercise will help you analyse the responsibilities in your relationship and discover your own and your partner's rights. By clarifying your rights and responsibilities, you can evaluate whether you're exercising your rights and meeting your responsibilities effectively. Knowing your mutual responsibilities and rights and keeping them in balance will help you define and express problems more clearly and recognise your right to be satisfied in each situation and also help you understand your partner's point of view.

EXERCISE

RIGHTS AND RESPONSIBILITIES ANALYSIS

Whether or not you are currently in a relationship, you can do this exercise. If you do not have a current partner, or your partner is not participating, just fill in the 'partner' columns as you would think your ideal (or current) partner would fill them in. If you and your partner are doing the exercise together, to give your discussion maximum effectiveness, do the columns alone first, and do not share your answers until instructed to do so in the discussion section, so that you won't influence each other's answers.

1 Divide a piece of paper in half, lengthwise, by either folding it or drawing a vertical line down the middle. Head one side of the paper 'Me' and the other 'My partner'. Under each name, put two column headings: 'Rights' and 'Responsibilities'. Your paper should look like this:

Me		My partner	
Rights	Responsibilities	Rights	Responsibilities

2 Fill in the column headed 'Me' first. Under rights, list all the things you see as your rights as a human being and your rights in the relationship. For example, your rights might include: 'the right to privacy', 'the right to feel what I feel', 'the right to work when and where I want to', 'to decide how the money I earn is spent', 'to go out alone with my friends', 'the right to ask for what I want', and 'the right to be heard by my partner'. Take your time and list at least ten rights.

3 Now, still in the 'Me' column, list what you see as your responsibilities. Include chores and work responsibilities as well as emotional responsibilities. For example, you might list: 'the responsibility to do the laundry', 'responsibility to listen to my partner', 'responsibility to earn enough money', 'responsibility to keep the peace', 'responsibility to keep myself healthy', 'responsibility to earn the family's living', 'responsibility to say what I want'. It's helpful to put related things in both columns, such as 'the right to be listened to' and 'the responsibility to be a good listener'.

4 Now, go to the column marked 'My partner', and repeat Steps 2 and 3 for your partner's rights and responsibilities *as you understand them*. For example, your partner may want the right to have separate friends and the responsibility to keep you informed about activities and keep commitments made with you.

5   *Evaluate your own list*   Now, compare your columns. Does it look balanced and fair to you? For example, do your rights outweigh your responsibilities or vice versa? If not, go back and add rights to balance each responsibility, or vice versa. Do your partner's rights and responsibilities seem about equal to yours? If not, go back and add rights to balance each responsibility, or vice versa. Keep adding to your lists, making adjustments until you feel your rights and responsibilities and your partner's are approximately equal. Ideally your rights and responsibilities and your partner's will feel mutually satisfying and reasonable to both of you.

6   *Discussion*   With your partner (or having a friend play the role of partner), compare the lists of rights and responsibilities. Make this an opportunity to increase your understanding of each other and your beliefs about the rights and responsibilities in your relationship. Ask questions about differences you have come up with, acknowledging each other's good ideas, and compare these lists to the actual rights and responsibilities you have in your current relationship. If you find that some of the things on your list are not present in your current relationship, discuss how adopting those rights and responsibilities would change things between you.

7   *Create a mutual list*   After your discussion, create a new list, with the rights and responsibilities of each partner, that you can both agree on. If you find yourselves struggling about a specific right or responsibility, use that as an example to practise co-operative negotiation with.

Getting clear about your rights and responsibilities in the relationship can give you the confidence to see that you do have rights, including the right to define and speak up about problems. You will also have a clearer agreement about your mutual rights and the reassurance that each of you recognises your responsibilities.

DEFINING YOUR PROBLEM

Now that you've learned how to overcome the barriers of confusion, shoulds, rebellion and compliance and secret expectations that may arise when you attempt to define and communicate a problem to your partner, *defining the problem* will be quite easy for you to do. As stated in the beginning of this chapter, there are three things to communicate in defining your problem:

1   A *problem exists*   The *problem inventory* will help you resolve any confusion you have and make you clearly aware that there really is a problem to be solved. The *compliance and rebellion inventory* and the *rights and responsibilities analysis* can also be useful in reassuring you that you have to ask for help with your problem and to strengthen your resolve to ask for the co-operation you want. By doing these exercises whenever you feel confused, you can learn to be more confident in your knowledge that a problem exists, just as Rose learned to in the example at the beginning of this chapter.

2 *What the problem is*   The final steps of the *problem inventory* are designed to help you become clear about what the problem is. If you still have some doubts or confusion about whether you 'should' feel the way you feel about the issue, reread the section on shoulds and creating permission, and use the *discovering secret expectations* exercise to break free from old stereotypes and assumptions that prevent you from seeing it clearly.

3 *Why your partner should co-operate*   In order to make your problem clear to your partner, you may need to explain (as Rose did) that if the problem goes unsolved, it will soon be a problem for your mate, too. The *rights and responsibilities analysis, compliance and rebellion inventory, creating permission, discovering secret expectations,* and *problem inventory,* added to the information you already have about why equal partners have more satisfying relationships, will help both you and your partner understand how both of you will benefit from co-operatively solving a problem, even though one or both of you have been unaware that the problem existed until now.

Once you have defined your problem and communicated it clearly to your partner, you are ready to move on to the next step in the negotiation tree – *agree to negotiate.*

CHAPTER 3

AGREE TO NEGOTIATE

Now that you are clear that there is a problem and you have clarified what the problem is, it is time to engage your partner to work with you to find a co-operative solution for it, to *agree to negotiate*.

Attempting to solve a problem without an agreement to negotiate means your intention will be unclear to your partner. If, when you brought up problems in the past, you found yourself competing, fighting, arguing, doing without, martyring yourself, feeling manipulated or exploited, giving in to keep the peace, or otherwise getting nowhere, it is probably because you began trying to work on the problem without a clear, mutually understood agreement that you'd work together to find the solution. Your partner may think you are complaining or criticising.

You can avoid struggling and fighting if you make certain your partner is prepared to work co-operatively with you. Getting an agreement to negotiate with your partner means you have a spoken contract that each of you will give your best effort and attention to working co-operatively to resolve the problem you've defined, to your mutual satisfaction.

This agreement minimises competition and struggling and encourages co-operation between you because it establishes the following important criteria for problem solving:

- it establishes that you are problem solving and not discussing, arguing, commiserating, or anything else;
- it makes clear your mutual commitment to work together to solve the problem;
- it is a way of communicating to each other that you are both participating in the process of negotiating;
- it helps you focus your attention on the task of solving the problem.

You've probably had the experience of bringing up a problem only to have your partner assume that your intention is to apportion blame, decide who is right and who is wrong, get your way at his or her expense or just generally complain. Without overtly agreeing to negotiate beforehand, you are more likely to argue because your intention to problem solve is unclear, like Michelle, twenty-four, and Ron, thirty-five, who struggle over who has the power in their relationship:

Michelle: *Ron, you treat me like a little girl all the time and it's really getting to me.*

Ron: *Well, you act like a little girl. You act so helpless about doing things around the house and about money. What do you expect me to do?*

Michelle: *There are some things you do better than me, but that doesn't make me your little girl! There are also some things I'm really good at and you still treat me as if I'm incompetent and unworthy of respect.*

Ron: *What are you complaining about? I pay the rent and I pay for everything when we go out! Do you want to start paying half of everything?*

Michelle: *Maybe I do.*

Ron: *Hah! That'll be the day.*

Michelle never mentioned that she would like to solve a problem, so Ron interpreted her complaint as an attack, responded defensively, and they never got beyond arguing. Michelle's problem of feeling patronised and demeaned is still unsolved (and effectively uncommunicated to Ron) and though Ron may feel that he won the argument, Michelle's resulting frustration and anger will make it difficult for him to get the intimacy he wants.

If Michelle had defined the problem and asked for an agreement to negotiate, Ron might have felt consulted instead of attacked and therefore been less likely to get defensive and more able to hear what she was saying.

But arguments can also happen even when one partner clearly offers to negotiate but the other partner has not clearly agreed to join in negotiating. Here Michelle clearly wants to negotiate and so does Ron, but he is still defensive:

Michelle: (stating problem taking responsibility for her part, but vague) *Ron, I'm getting more and more unhappy about how you treat me. My behaviour and attitude probably have something to do with it but I don't know what. Can we talk about it and see if we can sort it out?*

Ron: *I'm not happy about the situation either.* (not a clear agreement)

Michelle: (begins restating problem without a clear agreement) *When you tell people that I don't know something or I can't do something, I feel incompetent and uncomfortable. If you would give me credit for knowing what I do know and doing what I'm good at, I would feel a lot better.*

Ron: (defensive, not trying to co-operate) *Well, why don't you contradict me? Why don't you stand up for yourself?*

Michelle: (beginning to argue) *I don't know. It just seems futile, I suppose.*

Ron: *Well, there you are! You just give up! I wish you'd grow up!*

Michelle stated her problem and asked to negotiate. Then she proceeded to discuss the problem as if she had got an agreement from Ron to negotiate when, in fact, she had not. That left Ron free to avoid negotiation by criticising her.

In order to have an effective, successful negotiation, both of you must be committed to the problem-solving effort. Without a mutual agreement, you will probably wind up struggling instead of working together to find a solution.

This chapter will show how to be sure both of you are equally committed to solving the problem together and what to do if your partner won't agree.

Because this agreement is the first step toward making a mutual commitment to co-operative problem solving, there are more possible barriers to the agreement to negotiate than any other step in the process. In learning to overcome these barriers, you will learn most of the skills that end competitive struggles and make co-operation possible. This will make using the remaining steps of the negotiation tree much easier and speed you on your way towards a truly co-operative partnership. You can see the change in Ron's response when Michelle uses what she learned about defining the problem and gets Ron's agreement before negotiating.

Michelle: (clearly defining problem, and taking responsibility for her part) *Ron, I have a problem I'd like your help with. I often feel as if you're the one in charge and I'm your little girl. I know both of us are to blame and I'd like your help in solving the problem. We're both losing out if we can't be our real selves with each other and act as partners. I think you'd get a lot more of what you want if we worked together as equals and I'd like to see the little boy side of you once in a while.*

Ron: *And I'm tired of being the responsible adult all the time. Let's see if we can work it out.*

Michelle: OK.

Now that Ron and Michelle both understand the problem and have clearly agreed to negotiate it, the chance that they will be equally committed to solving the problem is much greater, as is the likelihood that they will successfully reach a mutually satisfactory agreement.

You don't need to ask for an agreement as formally as Michelle did, but it needs to be clearly communicated and clearly agreed to as in this example:

Fred: *Naomi, I'm really unhappy about our sex life and you seem to be unhappy lately, too. Let's sit down and see if we can talk it through.*

Naomi: *Yes, I'd like to do that.*

When you and your partner have a history of success in co-operative problem solving, agreeing to negotiate is quick, simple and usually easy. But, if you are new to the process, or you and your partner have a history of struggling or you come from a family where there was more fighting, rebellion or compliance than negotiating, it is not unusual for one partner to resist negotiating. You may have trouble getting agreement in the beginning because your (or your partner's) old, competitive habits will have a tendency to take over. Co-operating to solve problems is a new concept and because you are new at it, you may feel discouraged, awkward, or worried that you won't do it right. When partners are hesitant or feel hopeless about solving the conflict, they will not be as motivated to negotiate. Or, you may agree and then not follow it through. All of these problems are solvable and this chapter is designed to show you how to overcome these barriers to making an agreement to negotiate with your partner.

SKILLS FOR CO-OPERATION

*F*or most people, working together to solve conflicts is a totally new concept. Not only does it require a new way of thinking about problem solving but it also requires a set of skills which may be new to you. These basic skills are:

- trusting the process of co-operation and getting past your unfamiliarity with it, instead of letting your old habits take over;
- communicating clearly, with agreement-creating '*I*' messages, *active listening* and *attentive speaking* instead of conflict-creating criticism and defensiveness;
- reassuring each other, instead of struggling;
- persisting gently instead of giving up or getting angry; and, in the event your partner cannot or will not work with you,
- finding your own solution without your partner's help, instead of feeling helpless, dissatisfied and angry.

Getting an agreement to negotiate is the most critical step because no mutually satisfactory solution can be found if both people are not equally involved. Sometimes, agreeing to negotiate can be the most difficult step to achieve, because it is the point at which co-operation begins, and most couples are not familiar with solving problems co-operatively rather than competitively. Because of these difficulties, and in addition to exercises which help you learn the above skills and guidelines that you can use as you work together, we have created the *trouble shooting guide* at the end of this chapter. If you can't agree to negotiate, the guide will help you determine what your difficulty is and how to solve it. Related exercises and guidelines will teach you the skills you need to communicate clearly, understand your partner better, persist gently and overcome competing and struggling.

EFFECTIVE COMMUNICATION

*O*ne of the main keys to getting an agreement to negotiate is knowing how to communicate effectively. We have placed it first because it is so important and you will use it in every exercise in this chapter. Effective communication can help you overcome inexperience and mistrust, because you will be able to get across to your partner why co-operative problem solving will be beneficial to both of you without causing your partner to feel coerced or overwhelmed. It will also help you become more effective at *reassuring, overcoming rescues* and *persisting*, because all these skills require communication.

In fact, throughout the rest of the negotiation tree, since many steps of co-operative problem solving involve talking and sharing, the information and communication skills you will learn in this section can be used to solve many of the problems often encountered in problem solving. You have already seen, in chapter 3, that *how* you communicate your problem is crucial to being heard. Here you will learn communication techniques that will help you:

- keep your communication co-operative, rather than competitive;
- reassure your partner when fear blocks your problem solving;
- keep your conversation focused on getting information and solving the problem rather than defending yourselves.

THE BASICS OF COMMUNICATION

*E*xpressing your thoughts and feelings as facts about yourself ('I feel scared', rather than 'you scared me') leads to agreement because your partner will be more able to empathise and care about what you feel; expressing criticism of your partner ('you don't love me') leads to conflict because your partner will feel attacked and defensive.

Here are some examples of statements or questions that Michelle and Ron could use in their effort to negotiate about housework. Read the following parallel conversations and feel your reaction to the statements on each side. See if you can understand why we've categorised them under the two headings.

CONFLICT CREATING	AGREEMENT CREATING
Michelle: *You're condescending to me and I don't like it.*	*When you make a joke about something I do, I feel bad.*
Ron: *I'm just joking. Can't you take it?*	*Do you feel put down when I joke about you?*
Michelle: *Why are you such a bully? You put me down and when I complain, you put me down again.*	*Yes, I do feel bad if you make fun of me.*
Ron: *Look, when I tease you, I don't really mean it. You should know that by now.*	*I don't mean to make you feel bad. It's just that when you do something silly, I feel like teasing you.*

Michelle: *I think you do mean it. I think you want to punish me for being stupid.*

You feel you're teasing me but to me it feels like criticism. Maybe I already feel bad about it, so your teasing really hurts.

Ron: *Rubbish!*

Sorry, I had no idea it hurt you so much. I'll be more careful about teasing you. Now, do you want to get back to talking about the problem?

Michelle: *Forget it. I'm not going to talk to you.*

Thanks. I'll try not to be so sensitive. And yes, let's get back to the housework issue.

While it may seem difficult to make such rational, agreement-creating statements in the midst of a conflict, you'll see it is not as hard as it looks and certainly not as damaging to your relationship or difficult as dealing with constant conflict. If you review the conflict-creating statements, you will find they exhibit several attitudes:

- *defensive*   When you or your partner feels attacked, you'll be busy denying that you're to blame and not listening to each other.
- *argumentative*   When you focus more on who's right or wrong or whether the problem is real instead of focusing on how to work together to solve the problem.
- *objecting*   When you counter each of your partner's statements with a counter-argument instead of listening and trying to understand, or criticise your partner's opinion instead of listening.
- *critical judgements*   When your responses are about what's wrong with your partner instead of what your partner is saying.

All the above attitudes will be more likely to get a hostile, resistant response because they are negative and attacking, which prompts the listener to counter-attack. Therefore, the longer this conversation goes on, the more argumentative, and negative, and uncooperative it gets.

Both Michelle and Ron have a better chance of reaching an agreement to negotiate with the agreement-creating statements in the right-hand column, which have four elements in common:

- they demonstrate that you're listening because they reflect back what the other person said, which is reassuring to your partner, diffuses defensiveness and invites a similar, thoughtful response;
- they give or request non-judgemental, factual, 'I' message information;
- they are short and simple, so they can be easily understood;
- they are calm and thoughtful, rather than dramatic, emotional or reactive.

Because agreement-creating statements are calming, reassuring and informative, knowing how to use them in your negotiation can help you reduce the length and frequency of your arguments and power struggles. Because this type of dialogue minimises conflict and promotes sharing and listening, it allows each of you to learn new things about yourself and each other and makes your discussion more enjoyable. That means each negotiation makes the next agreement to negotiate easier because it leaves you with a positive feeling about the process and each other.

The skills demonstrated in the agreement-creating conversation on page 46 are:

- how to give information that is easy to hear and understand about what you feel and what you want (*'I' messages*);
- how to listen and play back what your partner said for confirmation that it's what was meant (*active listening*);
- how to make sure that the information received was what you intended to give (*attentive speaking*).

Learning these three skills can change your whole experience of talking from frustrating, volatile, argumentative and futile (conflict-based) exercises into calm, satisfying, effective and co-operative (agreement-based) discussions that accomplish what you intend.

'I' MESSAGES

Notice how the sentences that begin with 'I' in the agreement creating column on page 46 are easy to hear. It is much less threatening to your partner when you say, 'I feel hurt' or even 'I feel angry' than if you say, 'You hurt me' or 'You make me angry'. When you acknowledge that your feelings are yours, by saying 'I', your partner is less likely to feel blamed and get defensive than if you begin with 'You' (which focuses the responsibility on them) and more likely to be able to empathise and understand. By saying how you feel rather than blaming and accusing, you are much more likely to be understood.

'I' messages avoid the critical, attacking, defensiveness-creating atmosphere that 'You' messages create. 'You' messages consist of perceptions or judgements about the other person, usually couched in a critical, or even abusive, manner ('You didn't do that right', 'You look terrible', 'You made me so mad I wanted to hit you'). Of course, positive 'You' messages ('You're beautiful', 'You look lovely in that hat', 'You did a great job', 'You have a lovely smile') usually do not create problems, so it's only the negative, critical 'You' messages we're talking about here. Negative 'You' messages are seldom useful in negotiating because they are upsetting and they will probably make your partner defensive, which prevents him or her from listening or understanding.

Negative 'You' messages are very difficult to hear because when we feel criticised and accused we naturally get defensive, focus on counter-attacking and stop listening to the other person. 'I' statements, however, are easier to hear: 'I feel defensive' is easier to hear than 'You are attacking me'. 'I don't want to clean up the kitchen' is easier to hear than 'You left a mess in the kitchen'.

'I' messages are the most effective way to make yourself understood to your partner because you are communicating information about yourself in a way that minimises an argument. By using 'I' messages, you express what *you* think, feel, see and hear without projecting your feelings onto your partner – 'I'd like to go out with you more often', instead of 'You never want to go out with me anymore'. 'I' messages can be positive, too ('I love you', 'I feel great about the way we work together', 'I am very satisfied with this decision'). Sharing information about yourself, your feelings, your ideas and your reactions in this way helps your partner to understand you, your ideas and feelings.

'I' messages can also be clearer and more direct: it works better to say, 'I would like some time alone': instead of sighing and saying (passively), 'It's so hard to get enough time alone'. Or (indirectly), 'Don't you have to leave now?'

The following exercise will help you develop your 'I' messages skills, clarify what you want to say and make it easier for you to be heard by your partner when you have a problem or a disagreement.

EXERCISE

TURNING 'YOU' MESSAGES INTO 'I' MESSAGES

1 Review your relationship history and either (a) develop a list of 'You' messages that created problems in the past, or (b) observe yourself and your partner for a few days and record on paper any 'You' messages you hear.

2 Divide a piece of paper into two columns, as in the following example. Write the 'You' messages you collected in the left column and then practise turning each 'You' message into an 'I' message, as shown. Here are some examples to get you started.

'You' message	BECOMES	'I' message
You never take out the rubbish bin.	BECOMES	I want you to take out the rubbish bin as often as I do.
You aren't home enough.	BECOMES	I feel lonely and wonder if you still love me.
You don't spend enough time with me any more.	BECOMES	I miss the time we used to have together and I'm worried that you don't care any more.
You don't pay your share of the bills.	BECOMES	I want to renegotiate our financial agreement.

| Are you being unfaithful? | BECOMES | I feel insecure and suspicious because we're not having sex any more. |

'You' messages communicate that you feel angry, frustrated, critical of your partner or otherwise upset enough to say hurtful things and they make getting agreement difficult. If your partner is defensive, or uncooperative, notice whether you are speaking in 'You' messages. If so, use the above exercise to change them into 'I' messages and increase your chances of getting an agreement.

ACTIVE LISTENING

While 'I' messages will help you speak more effectively, active listening can help you hear your partner better. When you ask for an agreement to negotiate and your partner refuses, objects or avoids answering, active listening can help you understand *why* your partner is reluctant, so you can effectively reassure him or her and create the agreement you want. Active listening means paying attention to what your partner says, in the same way you'd like him or her to pay attention to what you say. To do this, you paraphrase (repeat in your own words) what your partner says to let your partner know that you are listening carefully and to confirm that you have understood what your partner meant, as in the following guidelines:

GUIDELINES FOR ACTIVE LISTENING

1 *Learn to recognise when your partner has something significant to discuss* While some people have no problem saying, 'I have something important to tell you', most of us usually aren't so clear. If you notice a change in your partner's emotional attitude or demeanour (for example, your normally talkative or cheerful partner becomes quiet, sullen or depressed, or snaps at you for no real reason, or is reluctant to discuss an issue or negotiate with you), he or she is probably worried about something. Let your partner know that you care about his or her feelings and objections by gently asking about it: 'Is there something you want to talk about?' or 'Do you have a problem with what I said?' or 'Is there a reason why you don't want to do this?' Ask, show your interest and caring, allow time for an answer, but don't push or insist.

2 *Do your best to pay attention to what your partner is saying* You know you have succeeded in understanding what your partner means when you can repeat what you heard and your partner confirms it. For example, if your partner says, 'You won't listen to what I want anyway', instead of arguing, just say, 'You believe I won't care about what you want?' If your partner says that's what he or she meant, you have just reassured him or her that you're listening. If not, keep rephrasing what you heard (or asking your partner to repeat it) until your partner confirms that is what he or she meant.

3 *Ask questions if you don't understand*   If your partner is going on at length, you might say, 'Could you stop a minute? I want to be sure I understand your last point before you go on to the next'. Then repeat what you have heard so far and get confirmation that you heard it the way your partner meant it. Don't allow yourself to become overwhelmed by a torrent of words or confusing statements; ask for explanations when you need them.

4 *Remember that listening to your partner does not necessarily mean you agree*   Even if you find that you still disagree, you'll have a better chance of solving the problem if you have a clear understanding of the opposing ideas. Saying 'Tell me more' is a wonderful way to be attentive to your partner when you are not sure you agree but want to understand what is going on before you question or challenge your partner's statements. You may find that you simply misunderstood what your partner said at first or that you're not as opposed to your partner's ideas as you thought.

5 *Take responsibility for speaking and listening*   If it seems to you that active listening means you have to take responsibility for both sides of the conversation, you're right, to a degree. Communication works best when both speaker and listener take responsibility for being heard and for hearing. While this may sound like a lot of work in the beginning, it will soon become obvious how much easier it is than arguing, fighting and not communicating.

Here are some examples of 'I' messages and active listening in action:

Michelle: *When you joke about a mistake I've made, I feel hurt and criticised.* ('I' message)

Ron: (paraphrasing; active listening) *Do you feel put down when I tease you?*

Michelle: *Yes I do.* (confirmation)

Carol: ('I' message) *I feel as if I do all the housework around here.*

Paul: (paraphrasing; active listening) *Sounds like you feel overworked and unappreciated.* (asking for information) *Tell me more about it; I want to understand.*

Don: ('I' message) *I'm going to start riding my bike to work on Thursdays so I can save time getting to night class.*

Peter: (critical, negative response) *It's too dangerous. That's a terrible neighbourhood and the traffic is awful.*

Don: (active listening) *You're afraid I'll have an accident?*

Peter: (calmer, confirms) *Yes. It's too dangerous. I don't want you to get hurt.*

Don: (asking for agreement to negotiate) *I don't want you to be worried. Do you want to discuss the problem?*

Peter: (relieved) *Yes. I'd like to have some say in your decision, too.*

Michelle: ('I' message) *Ron, I'm getting more and more worried about how we treat each other. I feel frustrated, unappreciated and criticised.*

Ron: (defensive) *Well, why don't you answer back? Why don't you stand up for yourself? I'm not doing anything wrong.*

Michelle: (paraphrasing; active listening) *Do you think I'm accusing you of doing something wrong?*

Ron: (confirming) *It sounds like it to me.*

Michelle: ('I' message) *I don't want to accuse you. I care about you and our relationship. I see a problem that could get out of hand and I'd like your help solving it.* (asking for agreement) *Will you help me sort out what's wrong and see what we both can do about it?*

Ron: (calmer, but still wary) *Well, when you put it that way, I suppose I'll try.*

Sometimes, active listening makes it clear that someone doesn't quite understand and this gives you the opportunity to clarify the misunderstanding, as in the following interchange between Michelle and Ron:

Michelle: (hurt, using 'I' messages) *When you joked about how I broke the blender last night, I felt embarrassed and stupid. It happens a lot and it upsets me.*

Ron: (confused, paraphrasing) *You're feeling miserable because I comment on mistakes you make?*

Michelle: (explains more clearly) *Yes, but it's more the way you comment. When you tease me, I feel like you're putting me down. It's an awful feeling.*

Ron: (catching on, paraphrasing again) *Being made fun of is the problem?*

Michelle: (confirming) *Yes.*

Ron: (offering to negotiate) *Now I understand. I didn't realise that my teasing upset you and I wondered why you were so cold to me afterwards. Do you want to see if we can sort it out?*

Michelle: (agreeing to negotiate) *Yes, I'd like to get it cleared up. It's causing us problems.*

Active listening allowed Michelle and Ron to avoid a potential argument and clarify what was being said enough to reach an agreement to negotiate.

ATTENTIVE SPEAKING

The third component of effective communication is *attentive speaking*. This is a technique taught mostly to salespersons and public speakers to help them keep the attention of their customers or audiences and make them more aware of whether they're getting their ideas across (so they can convince more effectively and thus sell more). It is a simple and highly effective technique that will help you communicate better with your partner, too.

Attentive speaking simply means paying attention not only to what you are saying, but to how your partner is reacting to it. If you watch carefully when you want to get a point across, your partner's facial expression, body movements and posture all will provide clues (looking interested, fidgeting, looking bored, eyes wandering, attempting to interrupt, facial expressions of anger or confusion, or a blank, empty stare) to help you know whether you are being understood.

By using the following guidelines, you can learn to observe your partner as he or she is listening to you and see whether you are successfully communicating what you want your partner to hear, without any verbal communication from your partner. This is especially effective if your partner:

- is not very talkative;
- thinks disagreeing or objecting will hurt your feelings;
- is the unemotional, strong, silent type;
- is easily overwhelmed in a discussion; or
- is passive, depressed or withdrawn.

Sometimes, such partners are reluctant to let you know if they have a negative reaction to what you are saying. If your partner is not interpreting what you are saying as you intended and you persist in talking without finding out your partner's feelings, your partner could become more and more upset by what you are saying, stop listening, get very confused, mentally object or silently argue with you, or not want to be talked to at all. If you don't use attentive speaking to spot the clues, you can be chattering blithely along and suddenly your partner will react with anger, misunderstand you or just not be interested in listening any more and all your efforts to communicate are wasted. By using the guidelines that follow, you can determine when you aren't communicating well or getting the reaction you want.

Using attentive speaking will help you:

- avoid overwhelming your partner with too much information at once (because you will notice when he or she looks overwhelmed, bored or distracted);
- keep your partner's interest in what you have to say (by teaching you how to ask a question when you see your partner's attention slipping away);
- understand when what you say is misunderstood (by observing facial expressions and noticing when they're different from what you expect);

- gauge your partner's reaction when he or she doesn't say anything (by facial expression, body language and attentiveness); and
- tell when your partner is too distracted, stressed or upset to really hear what you're saying (by facial expression, body language and attentiveness).

GUIDELINES FOR ATTENTIVE SPEAKING

1 *Look at your listener*   When it is important for you to communicate effectively, be careful not to get so engrossed in what you are saying that you forget to look at your partner. Keep your eyes on your partner's face and body. This will let your partner know you care if he or she hears you, increase your partner's tendency to make eye contact with you, and therefore cause him or her to listen more carefully.

2 *Look for clues*   Your partner's facial expression (a smile, a frown, a glassy-eyed stare), body position (upright and alert, slumped and sullen, turned away from you and inattentive) and movements (leaning towards you, pulling away from you, fidgeting, restlessness) will give you clues to your partner's reaction. For example, if you say, 'I love you', and you observe that your partner turns away and looks out the window, you are getting clues that you weren't received the way you wanted to be. Either your partner is too distracted to hear you or he or she is having a problem with what you said.

3 *Ask, don't guess*   If you get a response that seems unusual or inappropriate to what you said (you think you're giving a compliment and your partner looks confused, hurt or angry; or you think you're stating objective facts and your partner looks as if he or she disagrees; you're angry, but your partner is smiling), ask a gentle question – for example, 'I thought I was paying you a compliment, but you look annoyed. Did I say something wrong?' Or, 'I thought you'd be happy to hear that, but you look upset. Please tell me what you're thinking.' Or, 'I'm angry about what you just said, but you're smiling. Did I misunderstand you?' Or, just 'Do you agree?'

4 *Don't talk too long*   If your listener becomes fidgety or looks into space as you talk, either what you're saying is emotionally uncomfortable for your partner, the time is not good for talking (business pressures, stress, there's a good programme on television), your partner is bored, or you've been talking too long. If you think you've been talking too long or your partner is bored, invite your partner to comment: 'What do you think?' or 'Do you see it the same way?' or perhaps 'Am I talking too much (or too fast)?' If you think it's a bad time, just ask: 'You look distracted. Is this a good time to talk about this?' (If it is a bad time, then make a date to talk at a better time, or just begin again later.)

5 *Look for confusion*   When you're paying attention as you speak, lack of comprehension and confusion are also easy to spot. If your partner begins to have a blank or glassy-eyed look or looks worried or confused, you may be putting out too many ideas all at once or you may not be explaining your thoughts clearly enough. Again, ask a question: 'Am I making sense to

you?' 'Am I going too fast?' or, 'Do you have any questions?' Sometimes, just a pause in what you are saying will give your partner the room he or she needs to ask a question and get his or her confusion cleared up.

6 *Don't blame*   Blaming your listener – for example, by insisting that he or she just isn't paying enough attention – will only exacerbate the problem. Instead, ask a question, such as, 'I don't think I'm explaining this clearly. Have I lost you?' Or, 'Am I bringing up too many things at once?' Phrasing the questions to show that you're looking for ways to improve your style and clarity invites co-operation and encourages teamwork.

By using the guidelines above, you can find out immediately, as you are speaking, if you are communicating well with your partner. If you see signs of confusion or trouble, as Ron does in the following example, you can put things back on track quite easily.

After a busy period when Michelle and Ron haven't had much time for relaxation or with each other, they are in the kitchen getting breakfast before work:

Ron: *Michelle, I really do love you.*

Michelle: (looks out the window and says nothing)

Ron: (attentive speaking, asks for response) *Michelle, did you hear me? You looked away. Are you just tired, or is there a problem?*

Michelle: (angry) *I was thinking 'talk is cheap', but I didn't want to say it.*

Ron: (active listening, paraphrase) *Do you mean, you don't believe that I love you?*

Michelle: (calmer, using mostly 'I' messages) *Oh, I know you love me. It's just that I've felt neglected lately. You haven't been attentive, we haven't spent any time together and I've missed it. Saying 'I love you' isn't enough.*

Ron: (acknowledging, asking for negotiation) *You're right. We've been far too busy and I miss you too. Let's take some time off on Satuday from housework and things and sit down and discuss our schedule, so we can make more time for us.*

Michelle: (agrees to negotiate) *We do need to work some things out and it would be nice to talk. It's a date for Saturday.*

Ron's attentive speaking made him aware that Michelle didn't respond, and because of it, they were able to make an agreement to negotiate.

'I' messages, active listening and attentive speaking, can improve your communication so much that you can usually overcome most of the barriers of getting an agreement to negotiate, because your partner will feel cared about and listened to and will not be as likely to get defensive, competitive or argumentative. As you practise following the guidelines and become familiar with these effective communication skills, you'll find them very useful in all the steps of co-operative negotiation, in many of the exercises in the book and even in your conversations with friends, family and business associates.

BARRIERS TO AGREEING TO NEGOTIATE

*E*ven when you have good communication skills, you can fail to reach agreement because you encounter *barriers* – attitudes, beliefs and old habit patterns that can make it difficult or impossible to move through the various steps to getting an agreement to negotiate. At these times, one or both of you will seem:

- stubborn and unreasonable;
- hopeless and depressed;
- unable to communicate, even though you've learned the necessary skills;
- so afraid or anxious that you cannot be reassured; or
- unable to stop arguing and begin problem solving.

When these signs occur, you needn't panic or be discouraged. It simply means that you have encountered some of the barriers to agreeing to negotiate. You can learn to overcome each barrier and once you develop the skills presented in this chapter, you will find reaching an understanding with your partner much easier, even when the problem you are presenting is difficult.

The most common barriers people encounter in trying to get an agreement to negotiate are: *inexperience and mistrust*, the *power struggle habit*, and the *rescue*.

TRUST, INEXPERIENCE AND MISTRUST

*I*f you are both new at co-operative problem solving, neither of you will have enough experience at it to believe it is possible. As a result, you may have resistance to agreeing to negotiate. One or both of you may continue to argue, or be too busy, or agree and then not show up, or simply say no. The key to success is to allow yourselves to be beginners and learn the skills and have extra patience with yourselves and each other as you try these new ideas.

In the first dialogue in this chapter, Michelle was able to state her problem, but forgot to ask for a negotiation. In the second example, she asked but failed to notice that Ron had not agreed. However, after taking time to learn the skills of gentle persistence, clear communication and reassurance, Michelle could use these skills to enlist Ron in a negotiation:

Michelle: (clear communication) *Ron, I'm getting more and more depressed about how you talk down to me sometimes. I think we're both contributing to the problem and I want us to sit down and see if we can sort it out and find a way of being together that feels better.*

Ron: (shrugging her off) *That doesn't seem necessary. I'll just try to be nicer from now on.*

Michelle: (gentle persistence) *That's not what I had in mind. We tried that co-operative problem solving method before and I want to use it for this problem. It involves both of us and how we are together, so we need to agree to negotiate about it before we can go ahead.*

Ron: (resisting) *Seems like a lot to go through just because I criticise you sometimes. Why don't I just try to be nicer to you and let's see how it goes?*

Michelle: (more persistence and clear communication) *Ron, this is important and I think we're both going to have to make a change or two, and it doesn't involve 'being nicer'. I want to agree on the changes we are both going to make. Will you spend some time talking about it? I think it'll be worth it.*

Ron: (doubtful) *Sounds ominous. I don't know.*

Michelle: (reassuring) *I'm starting to feel like a nag, but I want you to realise that this is for us both. Remember that the purpose of negotiating is so that we both get what we want. We don't finish until we both feel good about the outcome. How about giving it a try?*

Ron: (reassured, agreeing) *You're very convincing. If you keep this up, I'll have to stop teasing you about not knowing anything. OK, let's give it a shot. When do we start?*

When Ron has successfully negotiated a number of issues with Michelle and seen that he gets what he wants, he will know from first-hand experience that the process works and how to do it. With practice, you and your partner will learn where you are likely to get into difficulties and how to remedy them. As you find yourself succeeding more often, your confidence in the technique will grow, making it easy to agree to negotiate.

Meanwhile there are skills (clear communication, reassurance and gentle persistence) that you can use to ease the way until you have your own successful negotiating experiences to draw on. We have provided sample dialogues throughout this chapter (and the book) as examples to help you through your inexperience phase.

OVERCOMING INEXPERIENCE AND MISTRUST

*I*n the beginning, you may have difficulty getting your partner to agree to negotiate because one or both of you lacks the experience of success with co-operative problem solving. Without an experience of success, the method can appear to be a lot of work with little or no benefit for the effort involved. If, like Paul in the following dialogue, you like the way things are, and (like Carol) your partner wants a change, you might refuse to negotiate.

Carol: (stating problem, asking for negotiation) *Paul, I'm feeling overworked because I work and do all the housework, too. Will you help me find a way to reduce my work load?*

Paul: (resisting negotiation) *Anything you come up with is OK with me as long as I don't have to do any housework. I'm much too tired for that.*

Carol: (asks more clearly) *What I want is your help in solving the problem. It's a problem that affects us both and I want you to participate in coming up with a solution.*

Paul: (refuses – shifts focus) *Well, I like* the way things are*, so it looks as if you're the only one with a problem.*

Because Paul and Carol are new at co-operative problem solving, and Paul sees no benefit to himself in negotiating the problem with Carol, he's reluctant to begin. If your partner, like Paul, refuses to negotiate and you suspect that it is because one or both of you doesn't have enough experience with co-operative problem solving, the *trouble shooting guide* at the end of this chapter can help you to understand where the trouble is, correct the problem and get on with your co-operative negotiation.

THE POWER STRUGGLE HABIT

For many couples, solving relationship problems has always meant a struggle in which one partner may 'win' the specific issue but both of you end up unsatisfied and sometimes resentful. So it's not surprising if one or both of you are unwilling to even try to negotiate for fear of reaching the same old outcome.

The struggle can be detected in the following patterns:

- *guilt and obligation*   This is the familiar 'If you loved me, you'd . . .' or 'How can you do that to me (expect that of me, not do that for me)' gambit. One partner uses guilt or obligation to coerce the other into doing something.
- *threats and emotional blackmail*   This is the opposite of guilt. Rather than saying 'If you loved me . . .' the attitude here is, 'If you don't do what I want, I won't love you'. In extreme cases, this can become very overbearing and abusive.
- *courtroom logic*   This is a relentless argument, lawyer-style, where one partner attempts to prove their case to show that they are right and deserve to get what they want. The argument sounds very logical but it is completely one-sided and does not take the other partner's wants, feelings and needs into account. In fact, it often belittles or dismisses them with logic.
- *keeping the peace*   Passive partners try to be nice and give in to the above manipulations to keep the peace by never saying what they want for fear it will upset their partner.

- *compromising*   *Both* partners give up some of what they want in order to reach agreement. It is time-honoured as the best way to solve problems, but couples who do it usually find that resentment builds as they give up what they want, bit by bit.
- *hammering away*   This is relentless persistence without gentleness or consideration for the other's wants, often called 'nagging', 'badgering' and 'harrassment'. One partner just keeps insisting on getting what he or she wants until the other gives in.

A competitive, power-struggle approach to problem solving is never pleasant for either partner. Even if the 'winner' sometimes feels good about getting what he or she wants, there are unpleasant repercussions later when anger and resentment build up in the 'losing' partner until it erupts in rage, depression or separation. So, if problem solving has meant struggle like this in your past history, it is quite easy to see why you or your partner might be hesitant to agree to begin the process.

When you ask for a negotiation, your partner might be suspicious that the offer is an attempt to manipulate him or her, especially if the two of you have a history of power struggles together. Peter, who is well aware that he and Don have a history of power struggles, reacts suspiciously to Don's offer to negotiate:

Don: *I've been thinking about your idea of using the back bedroom for your office and I'd like to use it for my office, too.*

Peter: *But it isn't big enough for both of us. What's the matter with your present office?*

Don: *I'd like to negotiate about this to see if we can both get what we want.*

Peter: *Negotiate? I don't know what I would do for an office if you had the back bedroom. Why do you need to give up your present office?*

Don: *If we negotiate, as in the book, maybe we can both be happy.*

Peter: *Not if you get that room and I have to stay in the dining room.*

Don: *Look, if I get the back bedroom and that makes you unhappy, then we haven't negotiated properly. Both of us have to be happy for the negotiation to be successful. Let's try it and see how it works.*

Peter: *I can tell you right now, I won't be happy if you get that room and I don't. No way.*

In the above example, Peter is clearly refusing to negotiate. At other times, the refusal may not be so clear. Here is how Peter might refuse in an indirect or covert way.

Don: *It looks like we both have our eyes on the back bedroom for an office. What do you say we try to find an answer?*

Peter: *I'm busy, not right now, sorry.*

– Later –

Don: *Do you want to talk about the back bedroom office situation?*

Peter: *I've got a lot of work to do.*

Peter is clearly saying he doesn't want to negotiate because he's not sure himself. He's feeling nervous about it, so he's just avoiding the subject in any way he can.

The guidelines and exercises in this chapter for overcoming the power struggle habit will show you how to overcome this natural resistance to struggling and replace it with confidence in mutual co-operation.

REASSURANCE AND OVERCOMING THE POWER STRUGGLE HABIT

When you and your partner, like Don and Peter, are accustomed to power struggles, your agreement to negotiate can be blocked by the fear that the negotiation will be just another power struggle, someone is going to lose, someone will end up feeling bad or nobody will win. Worse still, after all the hassle, frustration and resentment, the problem could remain unsolved. So, when you propose to negotiate, the response is, 'Why bother?'

If your partner responds negatively to your request to negotiate, it may be because he or she fears the outcome of the negotiation. Determining the source of the fear (is it fear of losing? fear of arguing or fighting? fear it won't work?) gives you an idea about what is needed to reassure your partner. Once you know how to reassure each other, as in the following step-by-step guidelines, you will be able to proceed with making the agreement to negotiate.

Reluctance or refusal to agree to problem solving is usually the result of one or more specific fears, such as:

- fear of being manipulated or overpowered;
- fear of being taken advantage of, or made a fool of;
- fear of having another fight;
- fear that the process will be a long, complicated hassle (hard work) without a worthwhile result (a waste of time);
- fear of losing or having to give up something important;
- fear that co-operative negotiation (because it's a new approach) won't go well or work at all.

Each of these fears, and any others that might come up, can be discovered, communicated and reassured, and the following guidelines will show you how.

GUIDELINES FOR REASSURANCE

1 *Find out what your partner's fears are*   If your partner won't agree to negotiate with you and you suspect he or she may be afraid of a bad outcome or wishes to avoid a power struggle, don't just assume you know that to be true. You will be creating a secret expectation, which will confuse both of you and increase your partner's resistance. Instead:

- tell your partner why you think he or she is avoiding dealing with the problem ('We agreed to take turns taking out the rubbish bin, and you haven't done your share', 'When I ask you to negotiate, you say you're busy');
- because you are using 'You', be sure you let your partner know that you're just explaining what leads you to believe he or she doesn't want to negotiate and *ask* your partner if what you see is correct and if it *does* mean he or she is reluctant to negotiate;
- if your partner denies that he or she is reluctant, ask again if the two of you can negotiate, since there is no reason why not;
- if your partner acknowledges that he or she is reluctant, let him or her know that you care about his or her feelings and ask what the reluctance is about. Whatever your partner says, don't argue about it. Listen to the answers carefully and use active listening to find out the reason for the refusal.

If your partner has trouble understanding what causes his or her reluctance, offer to read the list of fears on page 60 together to see what applies. It will help keep a co-operative atmosphere (and counteract the feeling that only one of you has, or is, a problem) if you acknowledge your own fears (as well as your partner's) as you read the list. To get fears into the open where they can be reassured, it is often helpful to consider what the worst possible outcome of agreeing to negotiate could be and allow your imagination to run wild (What if you find out you're incompatible and you have to break up? What if you get into such a bad fight you don't talk for days?). If either of you is having such alarming thoughts, it's better you get them into the open, where you can work out how to handle these unlikely events if they do happen. On the left-hand side of a piece of paper, make a list of the fears or fantasies that stop you and your partner from using co-operative negotiation. When your list is complete, you are ready to move on to reassurance, in Step 2.

Here's how Don uses these guidelines (informally) in response to Peter.

Don: (offer to negotiate) *Will you work this home office problem out with me?*

Peter: (avoids issue) *Maybe later. I'm reading right now.*

Don: (let's Peter know what Don thinks is happening) *Peter, I've asked you several times to work this out and I think you're avoiding it. Will you tell me why you keep putting me off?*

Peter: (begins to express fear) *I don't want to get into it. Why should I? If we talk about it, you'll just win the argument. I won't get anything I want.*

Don: (acknowledges fear by paraphrasing it, with active listening) *You think I'm going to try to talk you out of using the back bedroom?*

Peter: (relaxes a little, less defensive) *Yes. You've tried it before.*

Don: (more acknowledgement) *You're right, I think I have overpowered you in discussions before. And now you're afraid I'm going to try it again?*

Peter: *Yes.*

Don is clear now that the problem is Peter's fear (from past experience) that Don will overpower him. Now, he can proceed to the next step and reassure Peter about what he has learned about the importance of both of them getting what they want.

2 *Reassure your partner*   Avoiding a power struggle is avoiding something unpleasant. If you can reassure your partner that the negotiation itself will not be unpleasant, and it won't lead to something unpleasant, he or she will have nothing to fear. If your partner can be reassured that your negotiation can be a pleasant experience and the outcome can be very desirable, the resistance could turn to enthusiasm.

So, if you and your partner can't agree to negotiate because of your history of power struggling, reassurance will smooth the way. The following exercise will show you how to reassure your partner.

In Step 1 you determined your partner's fears. Now, you can begin to answer each one. To do that, consider each fear on the list and ask your partner what would reassure him or her and reduce the resistance. To reassure your partner, work out together how you would handle the situation if his or her worst fears came true ('If the argument got so bad we weren't talking, we could see a counsellor'). Knowing that you have a strategy to take care of yourselves if things don't go right will give your partner the additional confidence to try negotiation. If any of the fears are based on things that have happened before, acknowledge that they did happen and explain what is different now ('You're right, I did get angry and shout before, but I've realised that doesn't work and I've learned to control my anger better'). On the list of fears from Step 1, write the solutions or reassurances for each fear, as in the examples below.

FEAR	REASSURANCE
You're trying to manipulate me.	I have in the past, but not this time. I want to try this negotiation method and see if we both can really get what we want.

You'll try to overpower me.	The solution doesn't count if either of us doesn't like it.
We'll just end up fighting.	If we start arguing instead of negotiating, we'll stop and take a break.
I'll have to give up something.	If you don't like our solution, it won't count – and you can even change your mind later.
This is going to be hard work and a waste of time.	It may be hard work because we have to learn how to do it, but if it works, it'll make our life a lot easier.
I just don't trust this negotiation thing.	Since our solution doesn't count if we aren't both happy, what can we lost by trying it?

When you have reassured each fear on the list, you are ready to go to Step 3.

Once you get more accustomed to reassuring your partner, it can be done much more informally, as Don reassures Peter in the rest of their discussion from page 62:

Don: (more acknowledgement) *You're right, I suppose I have overpowered you in discussions before. And now you're afraid I'm going to try it again?*

Peter: *Yes.*

Don: (acknowledging and reassuring Peter's fear) *I can understand how you'd think I was trying to argue you out of using that room, because I've done that before over different issues. I know I've used anger, silence and shouting to win arguments before. But now I've learned some new ways of going about things and I realise that my old ways of winning have damaged the relationship. I want to try this co-operative negotiation where were work together to come up with a solution we both like.*

Peter: (still afraid) *Yes, but what if I don't like the solution?*

Don: (reassures again) *Then we keep working on it until we have a solution we both like.*

Peter: (not sure) *Sounds too good to be true.*

Don: (acknowledging, reassuring) *I know. But I think it's worth a try. We won't agree on anything that doesn't suit us both, and if we can't do it, we'll be no worse off than we are now.*

Peter: (one last fear) *Are you setting me up?*

Don: (one more reassurance) *No. I really want you to be happy with our solution. Will you give me a chance to show you, by trying a negotiation with me?*

Peter: (agrees, with reservations) OK, *but if you shout or get angry, I'm stopping.*

Don: *Right, it's a deal.*

Peter has been clear about his concerns and Don was able to respond directly, using the guidelines in an informal way. While Peter's agreement is not enthusiastic, it is a chance to try co-operative negotiation and let the experience itself prove that it works.

3 *Ask for agreement to negotiate*   Once you and your partner are reassured that you will not fall into your old power struggle habit, the resistance to negotiating should subside. Now you can begin again by asking for an agreement to negotiate and moving on to co-operative negotiation, like Don and Peter do here:

Don: *I really want you to be happy with our solution. How can I reassure you?*

Peter: *Show me, I suppose.*

Don: *Well, if we try negotiating, and I don't overpower you, will that show you?*

Peter: *Yes, I think so.*

Don: *OK, let's negotiate this problem of using the bedroom as an office.*

Peter: *I don't have to agree with your idea if I don't like it and you won't get angry?*

Don: *No, because I want you to be happy, too. As long as you are willing to try to solve the problem with me, I won't try to push you into doing what I want.*

Peter: *In that case, I'm willing to try negotiating.*

At this point, Don and Peter have overcome the major part of Peter's fears about power struggles, and they can begin by working together to explore the co-operative problem solving process.

As you practise reassuring yourself and your partner, you'll find it gets easier to do and the more reassurance you give each other, the easier and smoother your negotiation will be. Reassurance will come up again and again throughout the book, because it can be useful when you are having trouble with any of the steps of negotiation.

THE RESCUE

If, as a result of having learned only a competitive approach to problem solving and to each other, either you or your partner are accustomed to giving in, sacrificing or compromising as a way to resolve conflicts, you may derail the negotiation process before it ever gets started by not letting your partner know what you want or by giving in without negotiating, which we call a *rescue*. You are rescuing when you:

- give away all or part of what you want;
- attempt to guess or anticipate your partner's wants, without considering your own;
- try to please your partner, regardless of what you want;
- let your partner's real or imagined wants be more important to you than your own;
- give in before problem solving begins, as a way of avoiding painful power struggles.

People who view negotiation as a power struggle and want to avoid confrontation will avoid agreeing to negotiate if they can, so they rescue instead by doing the things listed above rather than by direct negotiating. A partner who rescues takes it upon him or herself to solve the problem by giving up all or part of what he or she wants or trying to anticipate what a partner wants and giving it before it's ever asked for. If you compromise, give in, or do a favour with a sense of sacrifice, resentment or superiority over your partner, then your action is a rescue.

Co-operative problem solving requires both people to know and say exactly what they want, in order to achieve mutual satisfaction. You are rescuing, not co-operating, if either of you avoids problem solving by giving up what you want. Letting the other person have their way may seem like being nice, co-operating or caring, but it leads to not getting what you want (with the resulting dissatisfaction and destructive resentment) instead of co-operative problem solving.

Rescuing and being rescued are such common ways for couples to act in our society, that it may sound like the way you 'should' be in your relationship. Often the relationships we see around us (as well as those in many books, plays, films, and songs) are built on rescuing and being rescued. Even though many people do it and many think they (and you) 'should' do it, rescuing and being rescued actually creates frustration, resentment and dissatisfaction in relationships and makes getting an agreement to negotiate impossible.

It is impossible to co-operatively negotiate with a partner who insists, 'There's no problem, we'll do it your way', or 'I don't really want to do what I suggested, I'd rather do what you want'. This is an attempt to be 'nice' but it doesn't allow both of you to get what you want. If you propose to negotiate and your partner just gives in, he or she is essentially saying no to negotiating. At these times, saying, 'OK, if you want to do it that way, it's fine with me', or, 'All right, I suppose so', can be the equivalent of saying, 'I would rather be dissatisfied than negotiate'. You or your partner can do this once in a while without creating a serious problem, but if it happens too often, it will leave the rescuer dissatisfied and resentful, eventually thinking 'After all I've done for you . . .' or, 'If you loved me, you'd . . .'

When Carol tries to get an agreement to negotiate from Paul, he puts up a rescue barrier:

Carol: (frustrated) *I feel as if I do all the housework and all the caring around here and there's no one to help me. Will you help me sort this out and find a solution that works for both of us?*

Paul: (feeling overburdened at work, but not saying so – avoiding the discussion at all costs) *OK, OK, I'll do the housework this week.*

If Carol accepts this as a solution to the problem, Paul will probably be in a bad mood all week, do the housework begrudgingly or badly, and/or 'forget' his promise, because he's rescuing to avoid problem solving and he has no real desire to help.

Another way to rescue is to not bring a problem up for negotiation at all. For example, Fred might say to himself: 'I'd join the Thursday night computer class, but it costs money and Naomi likes us to spend our evenings together, so I'll just forget it.' Without Naomi's knowledge, Fred has rescued her. If he does this often, he'll eventually feel that Naomi is restricting his life and he never manages to do what he wants and Naomi will wonder why he seems resentful.

Fred never asked Naomi how she felt about his joining a class. She might have welcomed the chance to have an evening to herself, to see friends or to take some classes on her own. She may have been excited for him and eager to support and encourage him. But if she doesn't say so, and Fred never tells her he'd like to take a class, both of them can feel restless, restricted and deprived. Neither of them will be fully aware that decisions have been made without discussion and both will feel confused at their own, and each other's, eventual dissatisfaction with their Thursday evenings together.

You can even rescue your partner by having a one-sided conversation out loud, as Carol does here:

Carol: *I'm exhausted tonight and I don't feel like doing the washing up. Can we do a deal?*

Paul: (silence. He's reading the paper)

Carol: *You're probably tired, too.*

Paul: (still silent, oblivious)

Carol: *What if I just stack the dishes and if you don't feel like doing them, I'll wash them in the morning.*

Paul: OK.

Carol has neatly argued herself into not asking for Paul's help in solving the problem about the dishes and, once again, left herself solely responsible for the housework, which she resents. Paul is content because he is getting what he wants and is not aware of Carol's resentment. However, by letting her give in, he may well pay a price later as a frustrated and angry Carol becomes grumpy, withholds sex or gets angry over small things.

Of course, not every time you and your partner agree is a rescue. Sometimes you truly agree with what your partner wants, so you are already getting what you want and a negotiation is unnecessary. If you feel satisfied, generous and loving, and want your partner to get what he or she wants and are not going to feel bad, deprived or exploited later, you are giving and not rescuing.

You can tell when it is genuine generosity, rather than a rescue, because the giver will feel good about it, rather than deprived or resentful.

The following section *overcoming the rescue* will help you become aware of when agreeing is rescuing and whether you or your partner are doing it. By identifying the related feelings and behaviours, it will teach you how to stop rescuing or being rescued and how to get an agreement to negotiate instead.

OVERCOMING THE RESCUE

If you feel dissatisfied or your partner seems resentful with your relationship and you don't seem to be able to discuss things with each other, then rescuing is probably your problem. The following checklist will help you discover if you are a rescuer or if you are being rescued and teach you how to change these destructive patterns so that you can have a much greater degree of mutual satisfaction in your relationship. After completing the checklist you will find further exercises to help you overcome either problem.

CHECKLIST: RESCUE DISCOVERY

The following checklist will help you decide if you are a rescuer or you are allowing yourself to be rescued.

YOU ARE A RESCUER IF YOU:
(Tick only the statements that apply to you.)

- believe you must do something for your partner that he or she can do for him or herself, without being asked or giving them a chance to refuse. 'I hate cooking, but Peter would starve to death if I didn't cook a good meal every night';
- do something that you do not want to do for or because of your partner and feel resentful later. (As in Carol and Paul's one-sided dialogue, page 66.)
- do not ask for what you want. Because you fear your partner's reaction to the request, you can't take no for an answer, or you believe your partner is incapable of saying no. (Fred's not asking Naomi about taking a class on Thursdays.)
- act as if your partner is incapable, put him or her in the child role and act as a parent. (Giving unsolicited advice, giving orders, nagging or criticising.)
- do not tell your partner when something he or she does or says is a problem for you; not asking for what you want your partner to do differently. (Rose resents John's bringing business associates home at short notice, but doesn't say anything.)
- contribute more than fifty per cent of the effort to any project or activity that is supposed to

be mutual (including housework, earning income, making dates and social plans, initiating sex, carrying the conversations, giving comfort and support) without an agreement that your extra efforts will be specifically and adequately rewarded or compensated;

- feel your role is to take care of, protect, control, feel for, worry about, ignore the expressed wishes of, or manipulate your partner. (Carol thinks she has to take care of Paul.)
- habitually feel tired, anxious, fearful, responsible, overworked and/or resentful in your relationship. (Ron feels overloaded frequently.)
- focus more on your partner's feelings, problems, circumstances, performance, satisfaction or happiness than on your own. (Rose is so concerned that John be content that she allowed herself to slide into depression without noticing.)
- feel let down, rejected, cheated, depressed, disappointed or otherwise dissatisfied by your partner. (Peter resents Don because he has allowed Don to overpower him in arguments.)

If you have ticked one or more of the above statements, you problably rescue and would benefit greatly from the *how to stop rescuing* exercise on page 69. The more familiar these feelings or actions are and the more frequently they occur, the stronger the habit you have of rescuing in your relationship.

The second part of the checklist is to determine if you often are rescued by your partner. Again, tick the statements that apply to you.

YOU ARE BEING RESCUED IF YOU:

- believe you are not as capable, mature or self-sufficient as your partner. (Michelle struggles to feel equal to Ron.)
- find that your partner is constantly doing things supposedly for you that you haven't requested or acknowledged (or may not even know about). (Fred didn't go to the class 'for Naomi's sake'.)
- feel guilty because your partner frequently seems to work harder, do more or want more than you do. (Paul feels guilty that Carol works *and* does all the housework.)
- do not need to ask for what you want because your partner anticipates your needs, or feel reluctant to ask because your partner will not say no if he or she doesn't want to do it. (Paul doesn't need to ask Carol, she does it anyway.)
- act or feel incapable, like a child, irresponsible, paralysed, nagged, criticised, powerless, taken care of or manipulated in your relationship. (Michelle often feels like a child.)
- act or feel demanding, greedy, selfish, out of control, over-emotional, lazy, worthless, pampered, spoiled, helpless or hopeless in your relationship;
- contribute less than fifty per cent of the effort to any project or activity that is supposed to be mutual (including housework, earning income, making dates and social plans, initiating sex, carrying the conversations, giving comfort and support) without an agreement that your

partner's extra efforts will be specifically and adequately rewarded or compensated;

- feel your role is fixed, protected, controlled, felt for, worried about, ignored or manipulated by your partner;
- habitually feel guilty, numb, turned off, overwhelmed, irresponsible, overlooked, misunderstood and/or hopeless in your relationship;
- focus more on your partner's approval, criticism, faults, anger, responsibility and power than on your own opinion of yourself;
- feel used, manipulated, victimised, abused, oppressed, stifled, limited or otherwise dissatisfied by your partner.

If you have ticked one or more of the above statements, you are probably being rescued and would benefit greatly from the *how to stop being rescued* exercise below. The more familiar these feelings or actions are, the more frequently they occur, the bigger the habit you have of being rescued in your relationship.

Rescuing is a habit that you learned early in life and you have done it for a long time, so it seems normal and is often difficult to be aware of when you are doing it. Rescues are related to secret expectations (except they are your expectations of what *you* should do, instead of what your partner should do), and rescues, too, depend on secrecy. You cannot be rescued once you have given or denied permission because you then have an open agreement, which can be negotiated, if necessary.

These exercises are designed to help you learn to recognise a rescue while you are doing it, making your unconscious behaviour conscious. They will help you stop and think about what is happening and how you are rescuing so you can begin to change that behaviour and change your rescues into proposals to negotiate.

EXERCISE

HOW TO STOP RESCUING AND/OR BEING RESCUED

The clarity you derive from doing this exercise will enable you to either avoid or get out of rescue situations; it is well worth the time and effort it takes to do it.

Choose a time and place when you will be uninterrupted. You will need a pencil and paper or you can discuss these questions aloud with afriend or your partner. By doing the exercise at a time when you are *not* having a problem with rescuing, you can reflect on your past experience and find the clues that will alert you to the next time you are tempted to rescue.

STEP 1   RECOGNISE A RESCUE WHILE YOU ARE PARTICIPATING IN IT

If, when you completed the *rescue discovery checklist*, you discovered or confirmed that you are more of a rescuer, you will find Part 1 very helpful, and if you discovered or confirmed that you were being rescued, Part 2 will be most effective for you. If you do both at different times, you'll find both parts useful.

Part 1 Review the *rescuer* checklist, to familiarise yourself with the ways you can tell when you are rescuing. Think back into your relationship history and choose a time when you felt the indicators on the rescuer checklist. Write a brief description of the events that were happening then and answer the following questions in your description.

- What were the circumstances?
- What were you doing (or not doing)?
- What was your partner doing (or not doing)?
- Was there a discussion? If so, what did you say (or not say); what did your partner say (or not say)?
- Did you have an internal dialogue with yourself at the time? What was it about?
- What was going on just before the rescue happened?
- What led you to believe you needed to rescue your partner?
- How did you feel about rescuing him or her?
- How did you feel afterwards?
- What could you have done, said, or perceived differently?

(Hint: If you are rescuing, tell the other person what you're tempted to do or not to do for them (how you want to rescue them) and ask them if they would like you to do that or not. Once you've offered and the offer has been accepted or rejected (even if your partner is not honest about what he or she wants or makes a mistake), it is no longer a rescue. It is an open agreement and can be renegotiated if necessary.)

Part 2 Review the *being rescued* checklist, to familiarise yourself with the ways you will know when you are being rescued. Think back into your relationship history and choose a time when you felt the indicators on the being rescued checklist. Write a description of the events that were happening then and answer the following questions in your description.

- What were the circumstances?
- What were you doing (or not doing)?
- What was your partner doing (or not doing)?
- Was there a discussion? If so, what did you say (or not say); what did your partner say (or not say)?
- Did you have an internal dialogue with yourself at the time? What was it about?
- What was going on just before the rescue happened?
- What led you to believe you needed to rescue your partner?
- How did you feel about rescuing him or her?

- How did you feel afterwards?
- What could you have done, said, or perceived differently?

(Hint: If you are being rescued, tell the other person that you don't need him or her to do that for you, and suggest negotiating or talking about it. ('Don, I know you think you have to cook dinner for me, but actually, I would like to get my own dinner sometimes, or even cook for you. Can we talk about it?') If you *don't* want to change what your partner does without asking, but just remove the possibility of resentment, thank your partner and check that it's really OK with him or her, which will change the rescue to an open agreement.)

You may want to re-do the above exercises using several different times when you were rescuing or being rescued, so that you can become as familiar as possible with the thoughts, actions and feelings that indicate you are involved in one side or the other of a rescue. Once you can easily recognise a rescue, you can move on to Step 2.

STEP **2**   WHEN YOU RECOGNISE THAT YOU ARE RESCUING OR BEING RESCUED, STOP AND THINK

After doing the *rescue/being rescued checklist,* and the two exercises in Step 1, you'll probably find that in the course of your ordinary, everyday interaction with your partner it will be quite obvious when a rescue is in progress. Now that you are aware of rescues, making changes is quite simple.

Part 1   Whenever you notice the cues from the checklists in Step 1, stop in the middle of your interaction and ask for a moment to think about whether you're rescuing or being rescued and what clues you are aware of. Tell your partner what you have observed, how you feel and what you think happened. 'I think I rescued you when I agreed to do all the weeding last week, because I feel resentful and I don't want to do it.' Or, 'I want to change my mind about agreeing to do the washing-up every night. I feel bad about it.'

Part 2   If you sense there are symptoms of rescuing but you're not clear what they are or what they mean, you can ask for a moment to think about it and review the following checklist:

- Are you contributing more or less than your share of the effort?
- Are you reluctant to say what you want?
- Are you wondering if your partner is honest about what he or she wants?
- Do you feel uncomfortable about the discussion you and your partner are having?
- Do you feel unsatisfied with the result?
- Are your trying to keep your partner from being hurt, angry, upset, sad or disappointed?
- Does this feel similar to discussions you've had before, where you felt bad at the end?

The more yeses you answer to this checklist, the more likely that you are involved in rescuing or being rescued at this moment. If you answered no to all these questions, you are probably *not* involved in a rescue. Continue with what you are doing. If you answered two or more questions with a yes, you probably are and you need to proceed to Step 3.

STEP **3** **PROPOSE TO NEGOTIATE**

Explain to your partner that you feel uncomfortable with the interaction between you and the clues you perceive. Ask your partner if he or she is uncomfortable too. Most of the time, if you are uncomfortable your partner will be, too. Discuss what either of you is doing that makes you feel resentful or unhappy, then ask your partner if he or she will negotiate with you.

In the dialogue earlier in this section, Carol asked to negotiate new housework arrangements and Paul volunteered to take over, even though he didn't want to. At first, Paul felt noble for helping Carol, but he soon realised he was feeling resentful and burdened, and that he was avoiding doing what he promised. Those feelings were his clue that he probably rescued Carol (*checklist*, and Step 1). He thought about the situation and realised that although he was fully understanding and supportive of Carol when it came to her feeling overworked and uncared for, he had a similar problem. He realised that he hadn't considered his own needs when he offered to do the housework (Step 2). At that point, he went to Carol and proposed to negotiate their housekeeping situation so that the needs of both of them could be met (Step 3).

Even though you want to give up rescuing or being rescued, your partner may not. If that happens, treat rescuing as a refusal to negotiate and use the *trouble shooting guide* (see page 76) to overcome it. Remember, even if your partner persists in rescuing or wanting to be rescued, if you state out loud what you believe is going on, you turn the rescue into an open agreement and open agreements can be discussed and negotiated.

GENTLE PERSISTENCE

Sometimes, no matter how good you are at communication techniques, how clearly you've defined your problem or how carefully you've asked for an agreement to negotiate, your partner will still refuse. This can happen whether you're new at negotiating or even after you have had several successful negotiations where both of you were completely happy with the results.

There are a lot of possible reasons why your partner (or you) could be reluctant or unwilling to negotiate:

- If your partner has never heard of co-operative negotiating or is suspicious of the process.
- If the problem is particularly frightening to either of you.
- If one of you is afraid of being manipulated or overpowered.
- If the problem seems insurmountable.
- If one of you is accustomed to being in charge.
- If the problem involves a life change.

If, for any reason, you have tried all the techniques in this chapter and your partner still refuses to negotiate, don't give up! Co-operative problem solving and the resulting mutual satisfaction and success are worth some extra effort on your part. If you've tried everything you can think of and your partner still won't agree to negotiate, *gentle persistence* is what you need.

Gentle persistence is the art of staying focused on your objective (solving your problem, getting an agreement to negotiate) and repeatedly asking your partner to participate, *without sounding critical, impatient, overbearing or dictatorial*. When it comes to getting an agreement to negotiate, gentle persistance can be a very effective and valuable skill.

Most of us only know how to persist in a nagging, complaining, whining or angry way – all styles of persistence that are based on the belief that the other person won't co-operate and has to be made unhappy or uncomfortable enough to give in to what we want. Gentle persistence, on the other hand, is based on a belief that your partner is a reasonable person who wants to co-operate, but somehow (even after all your communicating 'I' messages, and invitations to negotiate) hasn't heard you, misinterprets you or doesn't understand that's what you want.

Here's how Rose used gentle persistence to get John to listen to her:

Rose: *John, I want to talk to you.*

John: (offhand) *Fine, go ahead – I've always got time to listen.*

Rose: (stating problem) *John, I want to get a job and I want both of us to work out a way for both of us to be happy about it.*

John: (not believing) *Oh, Rose, you're not serious. What do you want, more money or new clothes?*

Rose: (still calm, explains more) *No, John, I want to get a job. I want to get out of the house and meet people. I want to have a career. Can we discuss it?*

John: (trying to distract her) *Now, now, Rose – why don't we just go out to dinner tonight?*

Rose: (still calm, more definite) *John, please listen to me. I'm serious.*

John: (looking for an excuse) *Is it the time of the month? You seem upset.*

Rose: (still calm, firmer) *I am not having emotional, physical or mental problems. I have made a decision about my life and that involves you. I want your co-operation. I want you to know I am sure about this and I will keep bringing it up until you agree to discuss the matter with me like two adults.*

John: (she got his attention with that, but he's sceptical) *I can see you are serious. But how can you mean it? The women in my family have never worked. My mother took pride in her house and children; she didn't need to work.*

Rose: (reassuring, still firm) *John, your mother was a fine woman. And so am I. These are different times. I want a new challenge. I know we can get your needs taken care of too. We can have help with the house and the children are grown-up. They don't need me. I need to feel productive again.*

John: (opening up, sharing fears) *But, Rose, what will my business associates think? What about our position? Who will take care of me?*

Rose: (reassuring, more gentle persistence) *I don't want to discomfort or embarrass you. Let's sit down and discuss it and I'm sure we can work it out. We're both intelligent. A solution that pleases both of us can't be too hard to find.*

John: (agrees) *Well, all right. I don't like the idea, but I'm willing to discuss it.*

Even though John is very reluctant even to consider Rose's request serious, her gentle persistence brought him around at least to a willingness to try. Such persistence may need to be repeated over a period of days or weeks if your partner is very reluctant to listen or has a difficult time understanding what you mean, but, if you can resist the impulse to nag or complain, it is very often successful.

When you gently persist, like Rose:

- You let your partner know that the problem you're experiencing is very important and must be resolved, but in a gentle, uncritical, non-threatening way.
- You gently but firmly refuse to give up your power to create good things in your life together, just because one of you is scared, angry or stubborn.
- You stay focused on your purpose and don't let yourself be drawn off course.
- You calmly and lovingly refuse to take no for an answer.

Gentle persistence is not as hard as it may sound and once you try it, you will be very motivated to do it because it works. The rewards for gently persisting are an agreement to negotiate, a mutually satisfactory solution and a relationship that works for both of you.

Read and consider the following guidelines. If you become familiar with them, they will help you keep your persistence from either becoming pushy and manipulative or help keep you from giving up.

GUIDELINES FOR GENTLE PERSISTENCE

1 *Be well prepared before trying gentle persistence*   Gentle persistence, especially when you're new at it, requires that you be in firm control of yourself. Choose a moment when you feel strong and you and your partner have some peaceful, uninterrupted time. You are demonstrating adult, thoughtful, calm and rational interaction for your partner, even if your partner is aggravating, dismissive or childish in his or her reactions, so you must feel strong and comfortable enough to stay calm and positive in the face of negative responses. Be sure you're not upset, exhausted, worried, or angry when you try it. You may need to let off steam elsewhere (in writing, to a friend) if you get annoyed, or drop the subject temporarily (and come back to it later) because you've run out of patience.

Understand that, until your partner realises the importance of co-operative negotiation in general or the importance of this particular issue to you, you are in the role of educator. Be sure you know clearly what you goal is (to get an agreement to negotiate about your problem). And be willing to explain it as many times as necessary, remaining calm every time. Rose chose a time when she felt strong and calm and waited until she was clear enough (using the *problem indicator inventory*, chapter 3) about what she wanted to discuss with John and she successfully remained calm, even when he seemed to belittle her.

2 *You both deserve to have what you want*   Gentle persistence is based on the conviction that you and your partner *both* deserve to get what you want. You're not asking for permission to have your way. You're making a firm offer to your partner to participate in the process so that he or she can have what they want also. If you maintain this point of view, you won't feel guilty, helpless, hopeless or angry. Remembering that you're working to create a change that is beneficial to both of you and your relationship, and even increases the odds that your relationship will continue to be successful, will keep you objective and motivated to succeed. Rose's conviction that she is doing something good and necessary for both of them shows in her statement, 'John, I want to get a job and I want both of us to work out a way for both of us to be happy about it'.

3 *Be gentle and firm*   Gentleness means treating your partner with respect and caring, while firmness means not giving in or giving up. If your partner says something, listen and answer it (with reassurance or 'I' statements) but don't agree unless it's meeting your objective. Don't slide into nagging, manipulating, pushing, coercing or abusing. Let your partner know that the issue is important to you, that you are serious about finding a satisfactory solution, that you want his or her participation in solving it and you're not going to give up or forget the idea. Rose used firm words: 'I want', 'I've made a decision'. She did not say, 'Would you like to . . .', 'I think I want . . .', 'Maybe . . .' or 'Would you be angry if I . . .'.

4 *Be sincere about co-operating*   Before you try gentle persistence, be sure that you really are willing to negotiate and that you honestly want your partner to be satisfied too, so that your invitation to your partner to participate is genuine. If you really desire a co-operative, equal relationship and your partner doesn't understand the value of this, it's up to you to lead the way. To succeed, you must accept the responsibility of being co-operative whether or not your partner agrees to participate. No matter what attempts John made to put Rose off or distract or annoy her, she didn't lose sight of her objective, get angry or disparage him.

5 *Try to understand your partners' resistance*   Any or all of the barriers (inexperience and mistrust, the power struggle habit or rescuing) can be in your way. Use active listening and attentive speaking to encourage your partner to talk about his or her reluctance and review the sections in this chapter on the barriers.

6 *Be as objective as possible*   When you express what you feel, use 'I' messages and don't expect your partner to agree. Instead, try to see both sides: why you want to negotiate, as well as

why your partner doesn't. The better you understand your partner's attitude and concerns, the more effective you will be at reassuring and convincing him or her that agreeing to negotiate will benefit him or her too. Seek to explain the benefits of negotiating as your partner would perceive them, through reassurance and active listening. Rose's statements, 'Your mother was a fine woman' and 'I know we can get your needs taken care of, too', were responses to appreciating John's point of view.

7 *Address your partner's fear*   You may need to reassure your partner many times while you are gently persisting, because you are changing the rules for how you deal with each other and change is unsettling and produces anxiety. Unwillingness to negotiate almost always indicates fear of the outcome. It can be very reassuring to remind your partner, as Rose did: 'I don't want to discomfort or embarrass you.' Or our old standby, 'I want both of us to be satisfied. I won't consider this negotiation successful or complete unless you get what you want too.'

8 *Remind your partner of your goodwill*   Love and respect usually reduce defensiveness and make co-operation easier. Take some time to remind yourself of all the good and valuable aspects of your relationship and then share them with your partner. Tell your partner you believe that, together, you can solve the problem. Rose expressed her goodwill at the end: 'I'm sure we can work it out. We're both intelligent. A solution that pleases both of us can't be too hard to find.'

With all the powerful techniques and guidelines you have learned about so far, the chances are you will have got an agreement to negotiate by this time and be ready to move on to the next step, *setting the stage* (chapter 4). But, in those rare cases where all the previous techniques have still not resulted in an agreement to negotiate, there are still some powerful remedies to try. The following trouble shooting guide will help you to understand why your attempt to get an agreement didn't work, and tell you what to do about it.

EXERCISE

TROUBLE SHOOTING GUIDE

This guide is intended to help you work out what techniques to use if you've tried everything you can think of but you're still stuck and cannot get an agreement to negotiate. The *trouble shooting guide* will help you now, when inexperience is your problem, and also later, when you both have more experience with co-operative problem solving, but you are unable to proceed or work out why. Returning to this guide will help you pinpoint how and why you are not getting an agreement to negotiate and remind you of what to do about it. You will find the guide very valuable as a reminder of what techniques to use whenever you have trouble getting an agreement to negotiate (which is often the most difficult step of problem solving), so keep it handy as a reference guide. Use it the same way you'd use a trouble shooting manual for a piece of complicated machinery: look down the list of problems until you find yours, then read the instructions.

PROBLEM 1   YOUR PARTNER DOESN'T UNDERSTAND WHAT CO-OPERATIVE PROBLEM SOLVING IS OR DOESN'T TRUST THAT IT WILL WORK

Many of the concepts and skills you will work with in negotiating will be new to both of you and if only one of you has read this book, the other may not know what is expected or intended. If your partner is interested in reading *Equal Partners*, you can discuss it together. If not, you can explain co-operative negotiating in your own words, why it is important to you and what about it is different from the way you usually handle problems. (Refer to *effective communication*, page 45 and *reassurance*, page 60.) Once your partner understands what you are proposing and agrees that it is worth trying, you can show him or her the negotiation tree and try again to define the problem and ask for an agreement to negotiate.

PROBLEM 2   YOU TRY TO GET AN AGREEMENT TO NEGOTIATE AND END UP ARGUING

Did you ask to negotiate in a way that your partner can understand? Find out if your partner has heard what you said and understands it. Make sure you are willing to listen to your partner's concerns as well as asking your partner to listen to yours. The more loving and respectful of your partner's feelings and opinions you are, the more likely it is that he or she will be open to and respectful of yours. Be sure you have used the clearest possible way to: give information about what you feel and what you want so that it can be heard by your partner; make sure that your partner hears you as you intend to be heard; and check, through listening and playing back what you hear, that you both understand each other.

PROBLEM 3   YOU BELIEVE YOUR PARTNER UNDERSTANDS YOUR INTENTIONS BUT HE OR SHE STILL WON'T AGREE

Your partner may not trust that co-operative negotiation can get you both what you want and you may need to resolve these fears. Or your partner may believe he or she could be taken advantage of, or that you may waste your time trying to negotiate, or that you will end up in an argument and damage your relationship. All of these reasons for not negotiating are based on fear. When someone is afraid to co-operate it is necessary to reassure them that they won't be harmed, cheated or degraded by the process and that you care about their feelings and needs, too. The essential attitude you need to establish in getting an agreement to negotiate is that both of you care about both of your wants, needs, and feelings and a negotiation is not co-operative unless both of you are satisfied with the result. Reminding yourself and your partner of this can make a lot of the anxiety and fear vanish and create an atmosphere where negotiation is much easier. The specific reassurance to give will vary with the kind of fear being experienced.

If you sense that your partner is worried, anxious or afraid, ask what the fear is about: 'Are you worried about something?' 'You seem reluctant to work with me on this. Will you tell me why?'

Once you understand what your partner fears, you can directly reassure him or her: 'No, I'm not trying to talk you into something you don't want to do. I care about your feelings too and I also care about mine. I'm trying to find a way we can work together so we can both get what we want.' Or, 'No, we won't argue about this all night. Let's try it for an hour and if we haven't got it solved by then, we'll make a new date to try it again. We don't even have to do it now. I'm just asking if you're willing to solve the problem with me. We can decide on a time to do it later.'

PROBLEM 4   YOU'VE TRIED ALL THE OTHER SUGGESTIONS AND STILL CAN'T AGREE TO NEGOTIATE

If you've followed Problems 1, 2 and 3 of this trouble shooting guide, and read through and applied everything in the chapter, and your partner is still unwilling, don't give up. Persistence is often the key to successful negotiation. Frequently, dropping the subject to give your partner time to think about it and then gently bringing it up later works very well. Especially if co-operative negotiating is new to you, your partner's initial resistance may be because he or she feels rushed or pushed, and needs some time to think about it before making an agreement.

PROBLEM 5   WHEN EVEN GENTLE PERSISTENCE DOESN'T WORK

When all else fails, the co-operative thing to do is to solve the problem yourself, inform your partner what your solution is, let him or her know you'd rather solve it together and leave an open invitation for your partner to join in co-operatively solving the problem at any time. Solving the problem to your own satisfaction, no matter what your partner may want, creates a great incentive for him or her to join you in negotiating, where his or her wants will be considered, too.

Here's how Carol, using the trouble shooting guide, persuades Paul to learn about and try co-operative problem solving:

Carol: (communicating clearly and inviting him to learn more about solving problems co-operatively) *Paul, I'm reading about co-operative problem solving as a way of tailoring our relationship so it totally suits us both. It's about how couples can learn to work together better, so they both become more satisfied and happy about being together. I'm really excited about it and I'd like to try it out. Are you interested?*

Paul: (not enthused, wary) *I don't know. What would I have to do?*

Carol: (offering options, reassuring) *Well, either you could read this book like I did or I could explain it to you as I understand it.*

Paul: (more interested, still not sure) *Sounds interesting, but do we need it? Aren't we doing fine already?*

Carol: (communicating, persisting, reassuring) *I think there are things in our relationship that you would like and are not getting and I thing this is a way for you to get more of what you want, and, to tell you the truth, there are a few important wrinkles for me that we need to iron out. I think this method sounds as if it might help us do that.*

Paul: (cautiously considering it) *OK, as long as you aren't expecting too much. I don't want to feel pressured to make a lot of changes because of some book, but I am willing to read it, if you give me a couple of weeks.*

– two weeks later –

Carol: (gently persisting) *Well, I know you read the book. What do you think?*

Paul: (still not convinced) *It sounds too good to be true, and also like a lot of work, and I don't know if it's worth it.*

Carol: (persisting, reassuring) *Paul, if it works, it'll be worth it, won't it? Remember my problem about housework? And I know you're not getting all the sexual contact you want. Maybe this will help us work these things out.*

Paul: (seeing some advantages to co-operative problem solving) *I see what you mean, but it still sounds too good to be true.*

Carol: (persisting, saying she'll solve it for herself) *Let's try it just a couple of times, and if it doesn't work, maybe we'll try counselling. I do think our problems aren't going to go away – they'll just get worse if we don't do something. If we don't try this, and you won't go to counselling, I'll have to go by myself and work on it alone. You won't be participating, so you might not like the result. This, on the other hand, is focused on getting you what you want too. Why not try it?*

Paul: (recognising he could lose out if he doesn't try) *OK, when you put it that way, I agree it's worth a try.*

When you obtain an agreement to negotiate, you are over the most difficult part of co-operative problem solving. The next step in the negotiation tree, in the next chapter, is *setting the stage*, where you will learn to set up and maintain an atmosphere that keeps your negotiation in a relaxed, positive, non-confrontational attitude of co-operation.

SOLVE IT YOURSELF

What do you do after you have tried everything and your partner still won't agree to negotiate? Up to this point you have learned many techniques for overcoming the barriers to agreeing to negotiate and most of the time they will work for you. If your partner doesn't seem to care or acknowledge that you have a significant problem, or is unwilling to help solve it, this section will give you the information and guidelines you need.

Like many people, you may believe you have only two options if your partner won't agree to negotiate: either you can attempt to change the other person's attitude through force or coercion; or you can give up. But there is a third option: you can choose to apply the steps of the guidelines on page 84 to solve the problem yourself. And when you have found a unilateral solution that solves the problem for you, you can re-approach your partner, stating your possible solution and offering to renegotiate. We call this *solving the problem for yourself.*

If you are faced with a partner who won't, or can't, negotiate with you, solving the problem for yourself bypasses all the struggle, hassle and arguing, and goes straight to the central issue: solving the problem. This is probably the most powerful encouragement for your partner to join in and agree to negotiate, because he or she does not get to be part of the solution unless he or she agrees. This is not done in a spirit of 'OK, you won't negotiate, so I'll show you', but in a spirit of 'I understand that you don't want to discuss this, so I'll have to solve it for myself, as best I can. When you are ready to co-operate and negotiate, I'll be available.'

There are several benefits to this approach:

- it is liberating to assert yourself on your own behalf and to realise that you don't have to have your partner's participation to be satisfied, nor have to shut him or her out, or be unkind;
- you no longer have the problem you were concerned about;
- you can still have a good, loving, relationship, because you have not done anything bad to your partner (if he or she doesn't like your solution, he or she can negotiate) and you aren't feeling frustrated, angry and deprived;
- it takes the pressure off your partner and increases the likelihood that he or she will relax and be less defensive or more interested;
- it prevents you from feeling helpless and frustrated, so you are more able to welcome your partner's co-operation when he or she offers it.

The key to solving the problem for yourself is a belief that you are entitled to satisfaction. Caring about your partner's wants and needs (as well as your own) is central to co-operation, but you cannot effectively meet your partner's needs without his or her help. Therefore, when your partner refuses to negotiate, he or she leaves you no choice but to focus on your own needs until he or she agrees to participate. As long as you offer every opportunity to co-operate and you extend an invitation to your partner to join you whenever he or she wishes, you are free to focus your attention on solving the problem for yourself. If you rescue and try to please your partner at your own expense, there is no chance for both of you to be satisfied.

The best solution is a course of action that puts you in control of your well-being, one that separates you from the effect of what your partner does or does not do.

Paul has stored up a lot of frustration because Carol has been late too many times, so he's decided to try solving the problem for himself:

Paul: (angry, but calm) *I've been standing here waiting for you for forty-five minutes. You said you'd be here at 6:00. Carol, this happens too often and I'm not putting up with it any more. I've tried to get you to talk to me about it but you never want to.*

Carol: (sheepish, not too concerned) *I'm sorry. One thing led to another and I lost track of time.*

Paul: (determined) *I've heard that too many times before! I am not prepared to wait like this again. It's too late tonight, the film's already started, so let's go out for a bite to eat and I'll tell you what I've decided.*

Carol: *OK.*

– at a coffeeshop, a little later –

Paul: (persisting) *I said I'd tell you what I've decided about being late, so here it is.*

Carol: (trying to change subject) *Ah, Paul . . .*

Paul: (persisting) *No, please don't interrupt me. You'll want to hear this, because it will affect you.*

Carol: (agreeing to listen) *OK.*

Paul: (firmly and clearly) *I don't want to be left waiting again. From now on when we make plans, I will wait for fifteen minutes, maximum. If you are not there in that time, I'll leave, so I don't have to get angry. If you call before our arranged time and say you'll be late and it's OK with me, we can discuss how long I'll wait. If we're going to a party or a show, I will leave a note and your ticket, if any, and you can join me when you get there. But I don't want to miss any more opening numbers or be late to any more films, because I'm waiting for you. Also, I won't make plans to meet you anywhere where I will be embarrassed or uncomfortable if you're late, such as having to sit in a restaurant, wondering if you'll turn up. Either we can go to the restaurant together or we can invite someone else along so I have someone to sit with if you are late. This way, I won't be angry and we won't argue about it any more. For my part, I will be clear about when your being on time is important to me and when timing is not so important. I will not be unreasonable about it. If I'm just pottering about at home and you're late, that's really not a problem and I won't turn it into one.*

Carol: (unhappy) *Oh, Paul, it sounds pretty strict.*

Paul: (standing firm, but explaining and reassuring) *It has to be, Carol, or I'll get so angry I won't see you any more and there's too much that's good about this relationship to let a simple thing like this spoil it. I love you, but I just can't wait around any more. It makes me feel unloved and uncared for, and that's not fair, because in many other ways, I know you love me.*

Carol: (resisting) *What if I don't agree?*

Paul: (offering to negotiate) *We can work out another solution together, one that makes both of us happy.*

Carol: (thinking about it) *Maybe that's a good idea. Let's arrange a time to discuss it.*

Sometimes, problems are more serious and solving it yourself is necessary to protect yourself, as it is with Carla and Ann. Carla, in the following example, is frustrated about the way her partner Ann deals with money, to the point that Carla's credit and financial security are being jeopardised – an issue that creates problems for many couples.

Carla: (concerned) *You haven't been contributing to our household account lately. You already owe me money from the past and for three weeks, I've bought the groceries and paid this month's gas and water bills. Are you in financial trouble again?*

Ann: (offhand) *I've had some expenses. I'll catch up on pay-day.*

Carlia: (not accepting that answer, persisting) *Your half of the current expenses so far is £120 and I'll need money for next month in the account – that's another £135 plus the rent.*

Ann: (still unconcerned) *OK.*

– after pay-day –

Carla: (persisting) *do you have the money for the household account?*

Ann: (casual) *I'm a little short. Here's £80 and I'll pay up the rest later.*

Carla: (not going along with her) *I'm feeling exploited. I want you to pay your share and you're not. I want to talk this through and get this problem solved.*

Ann: (denying) *Look, there's no problem. I'll sort it out next week.*

Carla: (persisting) *Ann, I've heard that before. I worry about how we handle our money and I want to work it out with you.*

Ann: (getting defensive) *I told you not to worry about it. I'll take care of it next week. Now, leave me alone.*

Carla: (realising she's not getting co-operation, asking for negotiation) *You don't seem to* *understand how concerned I am about this. I love you a lot and I'm worried about our relationship. How can we stay together if you're not paying for your half? I don't earn enough for both of us, and even if I did, it isn't fair. Let's sit down tonight and work this out. It's very serious.*

Ann: (refusing, changing subject) *Will you please just relax. Let's go out and enjoy ourselves. I'll treat you to a film tonight.*

Later, after considering the whole situation, Carla decides it's serious enough for her to solve it for herself. She decides to resort to a tough solution. In the midst of her emotional turmoil, Carla doesn't trust herself to be clear and calm in conversation with Ann, nor does she think Ann will take her seriously unless she writes it down. So Carla writes the following letter, which is a good way to be sure Ann has a chance to understand Carla's unilateral decision:

Dear Ann:

As you probably realise, I am very unhappy with our current financial dealings. I don't seem to be able to find a way to get you to see how important it is to me that you pay your share of expenses on time and without being reminded. I've attempted to discuss this with you, with no success. So, I've made a decision on my own. I've thought this through very carefully and I want you to know how very much I love you. I am very sad and frustrated because I can't find a way to encourage you to help me reach a solution that will work for both of us.

I've decided to solve the problem as best I can without you and here's my solution:

- *I'm going to buy food for myself only. I won't share it with you until we work the problem out;*
- *you have a good job and you make enough money to live on. I don't know what's wrong because you won't tell me, but your lateness paying bills and the rent is beginning to ruin my credit worthiness and I'm no longer going to pay your share. I'm giving you thirty-days' notice that if you don't pay your share of the expenses and the rent I'll move out. I hate doing this, because I like living with you, but it seems the only way to protect myself from your money problems.*
- *if that happens, I would still like to see you and be your partner, but without the financial entanglements.*

I want us both to be happy and be able to stay together, so if you want to work this out some other way and pay your full share, or at least tell me the truth about what's wrong, I'm more than willing to help. If you have a suggestion about how you can get what you want and I can still feel financially secure, I'd be happy to discuss it, but I can't accept any more empty promises. I just am not willing to feel used and taken advantage of any more. It's damaging my feelings for you.

With much love and some anger,
Carla

In the letter, Carla has taken a stand on behalf of herself and what she believes is her only chance for a satisfying life with Ann. Carla's solution is drastic, but very effective at releasing her from the problem Ann is causing. She knows that if this money issue goes on any longer, her good feelings about Ann will be destroyed and so will their relationship. In this way, Carla has regained control of her financial well-being and still left an open invitation to Ann to continue the rest of the relationship and even to renegotiate their financial arrangement on a more honest and realistic basis. Ann still has choices but she no longer can put Carla in financial jeopardy.

Ann has a good job, and makes enough money to support herself, so her non-payment is evidence that this could be a serious problem that requires a strong, tough solution. Even though Carla is horrified at the thought of losing Ann, she isn't willing to sacrifice herself and allow Ann's financial problem (and Carla's anger) to get worse.

This letter has an excellent chance of getting Ann's attention and achieving Carla's true goal, which is to work together on the problem. If Ann still won't negotiate, her problem is severe and Carla needs to protect herself by separating her funds from Ann's. At this point, Carla must allow Ann to make up her mind about what she wants to do. By putting their relationship on the line, while also continuing to offer to negotiate, Carla is presenting the strongerst possible motivation for Ann to want to deal with the problem and at the same time protecting herself in case Ann is so out of control that she can't resolve it.

If your problem is not as serious as Ann and Carla's, then your solution will be much less drastic, like Paul's, but the attitude of taking care of yourself while leaving the offer to negotiate open is the same.

In solving this serious problem for themselves, Carla and Paul followed several steps. By following the same steps, you can be sure you've given your partner ample opportunity to co-operate and you're not overreacting.

GUIDELINES FOR SOLVING IT YOURSELF

1 *Be sure you've made a thorough attempt to negotiate* Have you defined and communicated your problem, using all the techniques in chapter 2 (problem inventory, creating permission, analysing rights and responsibilities, and discovering secret expectations)? Have you used all the techniques and skills in this chapter in asking for an agreement to negotiate (overcoming inexperience and mistrust, communicating clearly, reassurance and gentle persistence)? To cover these steps, Carla opens her letter with a review of the problem and statements that she's tried to negotiate it. Review the problem and your attempts to solve it before telling your partner that you're solving it yourself. You can then open your discussion or letter as Paul or Carla did.

2 *Tell your partner what you are doing* State clearly that you have attempted to negotiate the problem, that your assessment is that your partner doesn't want to work on it, that you would prefer to work on it together but that you've decided what you are going to do about it on

your own. Carla writes how sad she is to have to resort to such a stern solution, Paul explains that he's protecting what's good about the relationship.

3 *Invite your partner to negotiate at any time*   Say, as Carla and Paul did, that you are going to follow your own solution unless your partner wants to discuss it, but that you are open to discussing it at any time if it makes him or her unhappy. This is your open invitation to negotiate at any time. It is important because it keeps the attitude of co-operation intact. Without the open invitation, solving it yourself can become a power play.

4 *Communicate your goodwill*   Let your partner know that you value him or her and the partnership, and you don't like having to make unilateral decisions, but you feel you have no choice, because you can't force him or her to work on it with you. Carla said how much she loved Ann and how she hated to do this, and Paul says he wants to protect his good feelings for Carol.

5 *Be sure your solution solves the problem for you*   Using the *stating wants and exploring options* exercises in chapters 5 and 6, find a solution that solves the problem in a way that's satisfying for you, even if you think your partner may not like it. If the solution works for both of you, the problem is solved and needs no further discussion, If your partner is not satisfied with your solution, he or she has already been invited to negotiate, and being left out is a powerful incentive.

A good rule of thumb in finding your own solution is to imagine what you would do about the problem if your partner weren't part of it. What would you do if you best friend were involved? Would it be different? Would the problem change if you lived alone or were single? What would you do then? Considering a relationship problem from the vantage point of a single person often points out places where you're being needlessly dependent. Because she was in financial jeopardy through her partner's refusal to co-operate, Carla's solution had to be financial disentanglement from Ann, while hoping to retain the emotional connection. If Ann does genuinely care and is not just using Carla for financial support, this decision will get her attention and get her interested in solving the problem. If not, Carla is at least saving herself from a disastrous financial situation. Before Carla made the decision, Ann's irresponsible behaviour was Carla's problem. Now, it has become Ann's problem. Paul's problem is less severe because it is just an inconvenience, but it still adversely affected his feelings for Carol. Paul's solution eliminates his feeling of powerlessness and not being cared about and allows Carol's problem with lateness to affect only her.

In obtaining an agreement to negotiate, you have learned to communicate what you want and how problem solving works to reassure and encourage your partner to participate, to persist gently until your partner understands how important it is to you, to overcome inexperience and mistrust by using the *trouble shooting guidelines*, to turn power struggles into co-operation, to change old habits of rescuing and resenting the result, and, if all else fails, to solve the problem yourself in order to demonstrate that problems can be solved and motivate your partner to be part of your solution.

Hopefully, you will seldom need to solve a problem without your partner's co-operation, but knowing you can solve the problem for yourself and still leave the door open to your partner's participation means you can remain calm and gentle in the face of a partner's reluctance to co-operate. This will certainly be better for your relationship than feeling frustrated, angry and taken advantage of. These skills create an atmosphere of co-operation between people and lead to negotiation that satisfies everyone involved. In the next chapter, you will learn the next step of co-operative problem solving after you do have an agreement to negotiate – *setting the stage*.

SET THE STAGE

Setting the stage is designed to make solving your problem as easy and efficient as possible. It will enable you to create the proper environment for effective and co-operative problem solving and further establish a mutual feeling of co-operation and teamwork by making sure you are both comfortable and available for uninterrupted discussion. While it takes a whole chapter to fully explain and to teach you the skills you need, you'll find in actual practice, setting the stage usually takes only moments.

Setting the stage consists of four parts: *choosing the time and place for negotiating; establishing goodwill ; reassuring each other*; and *setting aside held anger and hurt.*

CHOOSING TIME AND PLACE

Couples who do not set the stage properly, even though they've defined the problem and agreed to negotiate, can wind up feeling harried, confused, angry and/or trapped in negotiation when they don't have the time, the energy or the goodwill (motivation) to carry on. The resulting tension, if allowed to build, can sidetrack the negotiation into conflict and impede all the progress you've made in defining the problem and agreeing to negotiate, especially if you and your partner are new to co-operative problem solving or are negotiating a particularly difficult or long-standing problem.

Too often, couples who realise there is a problem may agree to solve it together but they pick a time when they feel rushed or tired or pick a setting that is uncomfortable, not private enough or has too many interruptions, or they are too vague about arranging a time and place and the discussion doesn't happen. The bigger and more long-standing the problem is, the more important setting a time and place becomes.

Poor conditions work against successful negotiation because they make it difficult to stay focused and think clearly. If lack of time, tiredness or a harried, anxious atmosphere interferes with your co-operation and problem solving, you can become discouraged and afraid that your negotiation won't work. Choosing a time when you both are rested and relaxed, when you won't be rushed or interrupted, stacks the odds in favour of successful negotiating. It allows you the time you need to think clearly and to explore, in a relaxed setting, all the aspects of the problem you are negotiating. Uninterrupted time will allow you to complete your negotiation as quickly and efficiently as possible and reduce tension between you. Properly setting the stage not only makes sure you have enough time and a good setting for uninterrupted negotiating, it also helps you establish the emotional climate of mutual caring and teamwork that is essential to co-operative problem solving. Without it you are more likely to see each other as competitors and be unable to work together co-operatively.

Rose, after working out how to define the problem and getting John's agreement to negotiate, agrees to put off the discussion until later because John has work he brought home from the office. Days pass and nothing more is said. Rose, who struggled to bring up the problem in the first place, feels reluctant to broach the subject again but finally she does:

Rose: (hesitantly) *John, do you remember when I said I had a problem about the children being gone and not having enough to do?*

John: (reading papers) *Uh-huh.*

Rose: (without much hope) *You said you'd discuss it with me.*

John: (distracted) *Not now, dear, I'm tired.*

Rose: (disappointed) *OK.* (gives up.)

– Now getting angry, Rose tries again the next morning –

Rose: (quietly fuming) *John, you said you'd discuss the problem with me and I want to talk about it now.*

John: (rushed) *Rose, don't pester me before work. You know I have to catch my train. I don't have time now.*

Rose: (angry) *Work, work, work! It's all you ever think about. You never want to talk about my worries. You love your work more than you love me.*

John: (angry, too) *OK, I've had enough! Don't you dare complain about my work. I've earned a good living for you and the children all these years. Just leave me alone.* (grabs coat and briefcase, leaves and slams the door)

Rose and John have just wiped out all the progress they made on the first two steps and now they're both angry. Why? Because neither of them realised how important choosing a time and place was. Rose picked a time when John was tired and he didn't realise that she was trying to re-open the negotiation. Then, because she was frustrated at his lack of response, she became impatient and anxious and tried to insist on negotiating at a time when John had to catch a train. He felt badgered and trapped, and responded by getting angry and leaving. They had an agreement to negotiate, but they had not done the first step in setting the stage and choosing a time and place that was agreeable to both of them.

However, once they learn to use this step of the negotiation tree, they are more thoughtful about when and where they negotiate.

Rose: *John, do you remember when I said I had a problem about the children being gone and not having enough to do?*

John: (reading the paper) *Uh-huh.* (puts down the paper, thinks a minute) *Oh, yes. We agreed to discuss it. When do you want to do it?*

Rose: (considering time and place) *I know you're tired now and it wouldn't go very well. What about having a nice dinner at home tomorrow night and then sitting down to talk afterwards?*

John: *That sounds good.* (agrees on time and place) *I'll make sure I'm home by 6:00. Will that be OK?*

Rose: (agrees) *Thank you. I really appreciate your co-operation. I'll make your favourite dinner – steak and kidney pie.*

John: (satisfied) *It will be a pleasure. We need a good, long talk and some time together.* (goes back to his paper. Rose, reassured, picks up a book)

What Rose and John have done is to choose the time and place for their negotiation. The following steps will help you choose a time and place more effectively.

EXERCISE

CHOOSING TIME AND PLACE

1 EVALUATE THE PROBLEM FOR TIME NEEDED

Consider the problem you are negotiating.

- Has it been long-standing?
- Does it seem that you are on opposite sides and will never agree?
- Are you able to think of several possible solutions or are you locked into just one outcome?

The more difficult the problem seems and the more insistent either of you is on a certain outcome, the longer it will probably take to solve the problem. The more relaxed you are and the more open-ended time you have, the more likely it is that the problem will be easily solved. So, if the problem seems difficult, choose a time and place that is open-ended or decide in advance that the negotiation may take more than one session. When you're new to co-operative problem solving, allow more time than you think you need. As you become more familiar with the process, your estimates of time needed will become more accurate.

2   CONSIDER BOTH YOUR SCHEDULES

Many couples have different schedules and preferences. One of you may be more alert and better-natured in the morning and the other more apt to be effective in the evening. Both of you may be busier at weekends (for example, with the children, washing, shopping, etc.) and more relaxed on weekday evenings after work. Or your work schedules might conflict. Compare your schedules and select a time that works well for both of you.

If one of you is more stressed about the problem, choose a time that makes it easiest for that partner. Experiment, and after trying a few negotiation sessions at different times, you'll find the best times for problem solving.

3   ARRANGE TO BE UNINTERRUPTED

When choosing time and place, remember that it is important to be uninterrupted. Turn on the answering machine or take the phone of the hook, find a way to occupy the children or see if a relative or neighbour will watch them for a while, and don't answer the door.

ESTABLISHING GOODWILL

Goodwill is a combination of the trust, affection and positive regard the partners have towards each other. People who like and respect each other get along better because they feel cared about, appreciated, trusted and caring towards each other. When you and your partner establish the goodwill you have for each other while you are co-operatively problem solving, you will have an easier time working together to solve the problem, because you will be reminded that solving this problem is a way to enhance the good relationship you already have.

Establishing goodwill reminds both of you that you are a team working together to solve the problem, rather than struggling with each other, helps you to remember that you both desire your mutual benefit and satisfaction and increases your pleasure in accomplishing something together.

Partners who try negotiating without establishing goodwill can forget to put the problem in its proper perspective to the relationship, see their partner as an enemy (competitor) and regard working on the problem as their only chance to make the relationship work. If that happens, in their anxiety they may compete, fear being taken advantage of, or fear that the negotiation will degenerate into an argument.

Rose and John, before they learned to establish goodwill, had many heated and frustrating encounters like the following:

(after dinner, at the agreed time)

Rose: (abruptly, anxious, not clear) OK, John, let's discuss my problem. I'm unhappy and I feel restless and useless. I can't go on like this.

John: (getting tense) *What do you want to do?*

Rose: (not problem solving, just reacting) *I don't know. I just feel unhappy. Maybe I should get a job.*

John: (back to his old ideas) *Rose, you don't need to work. I make enough money. I want you here at home.*

Rose: (angry) *You don't understand. I have to do something worthwhile.*

John: (angry) *So find something worthwhile to do! Don't bother me with it!*
(discussion ends with both of them dissatisfied and frustrated)

After Rose and John learn the importance of establishing goodwill, the dialogue goes differently:

Rose: (talks about good feelings) *John, I appreciate you being here to discuss this problem with me. You and I have solved a lot of problems together and I trust your advice and judgement.*

John: (lets her know he cares) *Rose, I enjoyed our meal and I'm looking forward to our discussion. You know that I have always wanted you to be happy and I'm sure we can work this out together.*

(Both are now reminded of their long, successful association and are ready to work together to solve the problem, which now feels more mutual.)

If, when you attempt to set the stage, you find that warmth and good feelings are not flowing between you and your partner, the following exercise can help you learn to express and develop your loving appreciation for yourselves, each other and your relationship. This exercise will help you draw on your relationship history to establish goodwill, so that you and your partner can remember that you're an experienced team, with a history of a successful and positive relationship. Negotiations are bound to go better when they begin in a calm, positive and hopeful atmosphere.

EXERCISE

ESTABLISHING GOODWILL

Although we recommend you always establish goodwill after choosing time and place and before the rest of the negotiation, you can use it any time the atmosphere gets tense or you get discouraged or worried about the outcome of your negotiation.

STEP 1   REVIEW PAST SUCCESSES

You and your partner, like every couple, have had successes, even if they seem hard to remember when you are struggling. You have had good times together and accomplished goals together. Perhaps you have had children, bought a house or a car, saved some money, gone to the theatre or dinner, celebrated anniversaries, survived illnesses, furnished your house or flat, renovated, painted and/or done it up together, visited family or friends, taken holiday trips together and spent weekends, days off, or holidays together. Remind each other of these good times. You will not only reactivate your loving feelings but you will be reminded of what is possible between you and why you are together today.

If you find yourself slipping into feelings of regret, hurt or anger because you don't experience those good times as much lately, see if you can return your attention to the good times and the loving feelings and go on to Part A. If you can't, go to the section on *setting aside held anger and hurt* on page 96.

Part A   Select three positive events   Select three of the positive events from you history, where you felt good about your partner and were enjoying the relationship. Go back in time as far as you need to, to find the good feelings: to the first excitement of meeting each other and dating, if necessary. Think about your three positive events for a few minutes and remember them clearly enough to describe them to your partner and write them down, if you wish, before going to Part B.

Part B   Share positive memories   Now, take a few moments to remind yourselves and each other how good things can be. Discuss your positive memories quietly and gently, until you feel some of those positive feelings towards each other right now. Whatever tension this problem has caused between you should relax as you share your memories and remind yourself that you're a partnership. When you feel a sense of connection and partnership, go on to the next step. (If you get stuck here, and can't reach your good feelings, use the *setting aside held anger and hurt exercise*, page 99 and then return to this exercise.)

STEP 2   ACKNOWLEDGE THE IMPORTANCE OF YOUR PARTNERSHIP

Neither of you would be even trying to resolve the issues between you if your partnership wasn't important to you. Remind each other that you care about the relationship and about yourselves and each other. You have made an investment of time, energy and caring in each other and in the relationship. Remind your partner what your investment is ('I have been with you for ____ years, and I want this to work') and that you care enough to resolve this problem so the two of you can go on happily together.

STEP 3   AGREE THAT A CO-OPERATIVE SOLUTION CAN BE FOUND

Although you may have difficulty believing that a solution can be found that will satisfy both of you, declare out loud to each other that there must be a way to co-operate in this situation and you intend to do everything you can to find what it is. State that you care about your partner being satisfied, as well as your being happy with the eventual solution, and that you know that both of you need to be satisfied if the solution is to work.

Establishing goowill usually creates the atmosphere of mutual caring, trust and teamwork that you need to feel co-operative, but if your problem is especially difficult, or if it is similar to a problem that caused major difficulty in a past relationship, or if you have a history of bitter struggles or fights instead of problem solving, you or your partner may still feel anxious. As we discussed in chapter 4, when one of you is anxious, that barrier can be overcome by reassurance.

REASSURANCE

Any disagreement between you creates tension in what is probably the most significant and important relationship you have, so both you and your partner are likely to be somewhat anxious about the outcome of your negotiation. Reassuring each other reduces this anxiety and, because you will both feel calmer, you will be able to think more clearly, be less likely to overreact emotionally and therefore co-operate more successfully. You will use reassurance again and again in co-operative problem solving, whenever your negotiating (or some other aspect of your relationship) becomes anxious, tense or otherwise difficult. One can never be too expert at reassurance. It is like a fine oil that makes the gears of a relationship turn smoothly.

Whenever anxiety or fear show up in the form of defensiveness, competitiveness, resistance to negotiating or tension between you, you can reassure each other by following these guidelines:

GUIDELINES FOR REASSURANCE

1 *Become aware of tension or difficulty*   If your conversation or negotiation begins to feel difficult, your partner is not being co-operative, or you find yourself feeling resistant and uncooperative, it may be time for reassurance.

2 *Verify and discuss the emotional atmosphere*   Suggest to your partner that both your feelings seem to need some attention and describe how the emotional climate feels to you. If your partner seems to you to be anxious, do not use 'You' messages to tell your partner how he or she feels, but use 'I' messages describing what you feel, see, or experience that seems uncomfortable. 'You' messages will increase the anxiety. If you think your partner is tense or anxious, ask for information.

   If Rose is aware that John has come home irritable, she can say, 'Hello, dear, how was your day?' This gives John an opening to express his tension or anxiety and for Rose to find a way to reassure him. Or, if she is aware that she herself is tense, she can say, 'John, I'm feeling anxious and stressed today. Will you help me understand why?'

   In the middle of negotiation, you might say, 'I need a break. This discussion has begun to feel tense and strained. How are you feeling? Are you worried about something?' (or: 'I am worried that . . .'). Once you have established and understood who is anxious or worried and why, go on to the next step.

3 *Identify and discuss reasons for tension*   The tension or anxiety between you or in the atmosphere will either be directly related to what you are discussing or it will be brought in from another source (work stress, an argument with someone else, bad commuting traffic). If your partner is anxious, use your attentive speaking and active listening skills to find out what he or she thinks and feels. Ask your partner if he or she feels anxious and if so, ask what it's about and use active listening and attentive speaking to find out if you are being misunderstood, as Rose does:

Rose: (opening discussion) *I'm really looking forward to discussing the changes I want to make in my life.*

John: (arms folded across chest, unsmiling) *What are we supposed to do to work it out?*

Rose: (asking for information) *John, you look anxious. Are you worried about this?*

John: (admits he's anxious) *Yes, I don't see how these changes will do anything but create problems.*

Rose: (active listening) *Are you afraid you life will change in ways you don't like?*

John: (confirming) *Yes.*

4 *Offer or ask for reassurance*   Once the source of the tension and/or anxiety is identified, specific reassurance is needed. For example, if you are anxious because you believe your partner is angry with you, you can ask to be reassured either that your partner is not angry or that the anger can be resolved and be told what you need to do to resolve it. Here, as in Steps 2 and 3, you will be using your communication skills to determine what reassurance to use. Sometimes the reassurance is spontaneous, as with Rose's response to John's fears:

John: (realising what he's tense about) *Maybe I'm afraid of losing you.*

Rose: (spontaneous, warm) *Oh, John, you couldn't lose me if you tried. I'll be with you for the rest of my life.*

John: (relieved, sighs) *Phew. That's a relief! I thought you were getting more independent so you could eventually leave.*

Rose: (more considered reassurance) *I promise, John, if I ever want to leave, I'll tell you straight out and not indirectly. OK?*

John: (much more relaxed posture) *OK. Now, I feel better about talking about it.*

5 *Continue until the atmosphere becomes more relaxed*   Depending on how long-standing or
intense the tension between you is, the above four steps can take a few minutes – or much
longer. Continue discussing the anxiety, the reasons behind it and the kind of reassurance
that is needed until you feel the tension between you relax. You'll be able to sense this
because the signs that indicated tension will change. For example, if you felt a knot in your
stomach, your stomach will now feel relaxed. Or, if you felt the conversation was difficult
and halting, it will now flow more smoothly. An atmosphere of heavy seriousness may
lighten into laughter. When your original indicators of tension are relaxed, you are ready to
resume the co-operative problem solving process. Rose knew John was reassured when he let
out a sigh of relief and his body relaxed.

If you are unable to reassure each other, or repeated attempts at reassurance don't seem to
help, suppressed hurt and anger from past conflicts may be coming to the surface. Try the
exercise for setting aside held anger and hurt and come back to this step again later.

BARRIER: UNRESOLVED ANGER AND HURT

If either you or your partner have had unsolved problems for a while, one or both of you may
have a backlog of suppressed anger, frustration or hurt feelings. Perhaps you feel that expressing
them would cause trouble or would accomplish nothing. These stored-up feelings can get in the
way if they come out during negotiating, because they create emotional and mental turmoil that
can interfere with co-operation and with clear thinking. Occasionally, held anger and hurt from
some other incident (last week's fight about an unrelated issue) can also interfere if it gets in the
way of your goodwill for one another and of your clear thinking.

Although your unresolved anger and hurt can emerge at any step in the negotiation, it will
most often be revealed as you set the stage and one or both of you have trouble establishing
goodwill and reassurance doesn't seem to help.

Setting the stage becomes impossible until held anger and hurt are resolved. Emotional turmoil
creates an atmosphere which interferes with your thinking and makes you see your partner as an
enemy with whom you are more likely to lapse into arguing or power struggles and turns the
negotiation into a competition.

It is inevitable that some hurt feelings and anger will arise in the course of a long-term
relationship. Learning to set aside these intense feelings when you negotiate is a very useful skill
that will benefit you and your partner in many situations in addition to your negotiations,
including at work, when problems arise with your children or when emergencies must be handled
in spite of intense feelings.

If Rose has been struggling with her discontent for some time and has had trouble getting John to take her seriously, she could have several months or even a year or two of hurt and resentment stored up about it:

John: *Well, this is our negotiation date.* (establishing goodwill) *I love you, Rose, and I want to do what I can to make our life together the best it can be for both of us.*

Rose: (bitterly) *Yes, as long as it doesn't upset your tidy little nest.*

John: (startled) *If you can't be civil, I don't want to discuss it.*

Rose: (angry) *That's just your style. If it doesn't suit you, you refuse to talk!*

(end of discussion)

On the other hand, if Rose and John know about setting aside held anger and hurt, the evening can take quite another turn:

(a little later)

Rose: (thoughtful) *John, I'm sorry I blew up a while ago. I took time to write and think about it, and I realised that I've been blaming you for my discontent and resentment that you wouldn't help me work out my problem. I'm not angry now. In fact, I appreciate your trying to open the negotiation tonight, when it's my problem.*

John: (cautious) *I didn't realise you were so upset. Maybe we can try again, but I think we both need a little more time to settle down and cool down. Can we wait fifteen minutes and then come back to it?*

Rose: (agreeing) *I think that's a good idea. Let's have our coffee, and then try again.*

Rose's held anger had been building for a while and after it erupted, she took a break and wrote in her journal and thought about it. Once she had worked through her held anger, she was able to come back and explain herself to John and ask to resume the negotiation. John had been taken by surprise and his anger didn't last long, so after requesting a short additional break, he's ready to go again.

SETTING ASIDE HELD ANGER AND HURT

*I*f you or your partner are holding anger or hurt feelings regarding the problem you want to solve, or for any other reason, before you can proceed in your negotiation, a period of emotional discharge may be necessary. This discharge may be as simple as saying, 'Wait a minute. I'm still angry about this and I have to re-focus on what we're doing.' Or, if your anger and frustration has been long-standing, it may require taking a break in the negotiation at this point for the purpose of discharging or *setting aside held anger and hurt*. Also, it's important to remember that discharging your anger away from the person you're upset with allows you to express your feelings in a way that doesn't aggravate the problem, and once your feelings are dealt with, you will be calm and able to think clearly enough to return to your partner and solve the problem.

You and your partner can learn how to take time away from the problem to release and resolve anger, frustration and hurt feelings in a variety of ways:

- putting it aside temporarily by changing focus;
- releasing your anger and hurt through physical activity;
- releasing your anger and hurt by expressing your feelings through writing or talking; or
- releasing it by talking with a friend or psychotherapist who will listen.

Depending on the intensity of your held hurt and anger, how long-standing it is and how comfortable you are with handling your feelings, you can choose to discharge it by yourself or with the help of another. Whichever you choose, remember, the partner who helped you generate the anger and hurt in the first place will probably not be able to listen objectively enough to help you discharge it.

DISCHARGING ANGER BY YOURSELF

Common levels of held anger or hurt (because they are not too overwhelming) can be discharged alone by writing down your feelings, talking out loud to yourself and simply acknowledging how you feel as in the directions below. Many people think that feelings can only be discharged by talking them out with someone else (as in the directions here) and this is fine if you happen to have an appropriate friend handy when you need them or are in therapy. But learning to discharge your anger by yourself keeps you from being over dependent on others and is usually much simpler and less of an interruption in your problem solving.

The advantages to releasing your held anger and hurt alone are:

- you can do it when and where you want instead of waiting for the right friend or therapist to be available;
- it is simpler than making arrangements with another person;
- it may be easier to be more honest about your hurt and anger to yourself than to another;
- you can choose a method that suits your personality and the nature of your problem; and
- it doesn't postpone your negotiation as much as making arrangements to talk to someone else does.

We recommend trying to discharge your anger by yourself first, using the guidelines below, and if you find that your held anger and hurt are too intense for you to handle alone, then get the help of a friend or psychotherapist.

DISCHARGING ANGER WITH A FRIEND

Some people find it easier to release feelings by talking to someone, because they feel heard, cared about and validated, and they have someone's implicit permission to discharge their anger. Also, since your friend is uninvolved in the problem, you know that your anger or hurt won't place pressure on or upset him or her. Very few good friends are objective enough to be good listeners, so when you choose someone, make sure they can hear you without passing judgement. The listener's role is to be nonjudgemental, dispassionate and supportive. Also, you must be very careful which friend you choose to share your feelings with. Because you will be talking about your anger and hurt towards your partner, you need a friend who can understand that the feelings are temporary. Speak to someone who will listen to you without placing blame on either you or your partner and who won't create problems by repeating what you said or bring it up later.

If attempting to discharge on your own doesn't help, call a friend, read the above description of a good listener and see if he or she will agree to help you. Then follow the instructions in the guidelines below.

DISCHARGING ANGER WITH PROFESSIONAL HELP

In cases where emotions have been pent-up for a long time or involve repeated negative patterns (such as being abandoned, financially devastated or cheated on) from past relationships, or in which rape, violence, child abuse or other traumatic history is involved, discharging held hurt and anger is critically important, needs knowledgeable supervision and can take some time to complete. In these cases, getting into group or individual therapy is essential. If this describes you, and you are not in therapy, get a referral from a friend, a doctor, or contact one of the organisations listed in the appendix. Your therapist will help you follow the guidelines below or use similar methods of discharging your anger.

GUIDELINES FOR SETTING ASIDE HELD ANGER AND HURT

1 *Separate from the problem*   In order to discharge anger effectively, explain that you have held hurt and anger, request a break from problem solving and find a secure place to be alone or with an uninvolved, neutral person. As we said above, this should be done away from your partner. To request a break in the negotiation, state that you're too angry, hurt or tense to continue right now, and you want a break to take care of your feelings first. Set a new time and palce to resume the discussion later, even another day if necessary, which will reassure your partner that the negotiation will continue and that you are not using your hurt and anger to avoid negotiating permanently. Allow plenty of time to discharge your held feelings in one of the following ways. You can choose to do each of these options alone or with a friend or therapist, as previously explained.

2 *Choose a method*   There are three methods of setting aside held anger and hurt, each of which is outlined in the exercises that follow. To choose the appropriate exercise for you, use the following guidelines, which include simple exercises:

A   TEMPORARILY SETTING FEELINGS ASIDE   This is the simplest of the options. John, for example, was able to take a few minutes' break, let his surprise and hurt subside, and simply focus on the negotiation again, because his hurt wasn't long-standing or deep but was a result of his conflict and misunderstanding with Rose earlier that same evening.

You may find it relatively easy to postpone dealing with your feelings and stay focused on problem solving, with just a short (five- to fifteen-minute) break. The deeper and more intense the feelings are and the less experienced you are at managing your feelings, the more difficult this is to do, so this is the best option to choose for a small upset.

EXERCISE A

TEMPORARILY SETTING FEELINGS ASIDE

This exercise is done by yourself, in your own mind:

1 Focus your mind, notice what you are feeling and acknowledge that it is an appropriate feeling.
2 See if you can set it aside for now (postpone expressing it) and continue the negotiation.
3 If you decide to postpone expressing it, focus on something that will motivate you to return to the discussion, such as your desire to resolve the problem you are negotiating or your respect and love for your partner. Allow the anger or hurt to fade into the background as you move your attention to the task at hand.
4 Go on to Step 3 of these guidelines on page 100.

B   RELEASE THROUGH PHYSICAL ACTIVITY   Choose this option if you enjoy physical activity and you often experience a change of mood after exercising. Emotions that are pent up can often be released through physical activity, such as a brisk walk, dancing to music with a steady, pulsing beat, bicycling, jogging, Tai Chi, yoga, swimming, wrestling, punching a pillow or a punchbag, or throwing something repeatedly in a safe setting. (A large, heavy phone book or catalogue thrown at a soft bed or couch is energetic and safe, as is throwing or hitting a ball against a wall as in tennis or squash, or beating a mattress with a tennis raquet or a bat.)

When you begin your 'workout' you may feel your held emotion as tension in your body, usually in the stomach, chest, shoulders, back, neck, head or jaws. The exercise will loosen the muscles holding the tension and allow you to release some of the held emotion so you can get back to negotiating.

EXERCISE B

RELEASE THROUGH PHYSICAL ACTIVITY

1 Choose an exercise from the above examples or your favourite physical activity and set aside a time to handle these feelings through the activity.

2 As you exercise, pay attention to your feelings and whatever tension you feel in your body and try to continue your workout until the intensity of your hurt and anger are reduced and you can re-connect with the good feelings you have towards your partner and can focus on the task of problem solving.

3 Go to Step 3 of these guidelines, below.

C   RELEASE THROUGH VERBAL OR WRITTEN EXPRESSION   Choose this option if you often use writing or talking out loud (to yourself or to a friend) to help you understand how you feel and what you want to do. Held emotions are exactly that – held. When you express them they lose their pent-up energy and become much easier to deal with and set aside. You may find *Breaking Free From Your Past*, another title in this series, useful in helping you to do this.

EXERCISE C

RELEASE THROUGH VERBAL OR WRITTEN EXPRESSION

1 Find a place to be alone and uninterrupted for whatever time you need to write out or talk through your feelings. Your held anger and hurt can be expressed in whatever way feels best to you – write, shout, talk or cry. The more you allow yourself to express what you are angry or hurt about, the easier it will be to let those feelings go and get on to the business of solving the problem.

2 Once you have written or talked enough to understand your feelings and decide what to do about them, go to Step 3 of the guidelines.

3 *Wait for a release*   Keep expressing your feelings in your chosen way until you feel a letting go or release. This is the discharge and you'll know when you get to it because you'll experience a feeling of relief. Along with the relief, you may also discover the real or central reason for the feelings, which often spontaneously comes in the form of a new idea. It is often accompanied by a feeling of discovery or relief. For example, John told himself how angry he was while he took a shower and after a few minutes, he suddenly realised, 'Oh! I'm angry at Rose because she surprised me by being angry when I was ready to negotiate and feeling my love for her. I felt ambushed. When she apologised, I wasn't ready to forgive her. I think I'm ready now because it doesn't seem so important any more.'

When you feel your tension release, you'll find that your thinking capacity returns and you can go on with problem solving, either by yourself or with the other person. You will now be able to think clearly enough to use your autonomous thinking and effective choice making to solve the problem, so you are ready to resume negotiating as you agreed.

Mastering these skills will enable you to create a calm, mutually caring, co-operative and inviting atmosphere in which it will be easy to think clearly and solve the problem. Being able to create this atmosphere whenever you want to is a valuable skill that will greatly enhance your co-operative problem solving efforts.

You are now ready to move on to the final phases of co-operative negotiation. In the next chapter, you will learn about *stating your wants*, a key step of the negotiation tree, where you and your partner communicate exactly what you want. This is the step where you will become clear about where you are in agreement and where you are in conflict.

CHAPTER 5

STATE YOUR WANTS

Once you have set the stage, you and your partner can focus on solving the problem, as a team, without being distracted by old anger and hurt or by interruptions. *Stating and exploring wants* is the first step of the negotiation tree where you *both* begin to contribute to the problem-solving process, by participating equally in stating what you want.

Stating wants in a helpful, non-threatening way is critical to solving the problem because it helps both you and your partner understand the differences and similarities in the way you want this problem solved and what it will take to satisfy each of you. If you don't know what your partner wants, you can wind up with a false, or one-sided, solution that will leave one or both of you feeling unsatisfied, overpowered or manipulated. Stating wants is like putting all the true facts on the table, just as you lay all the pieces of a jigsaw puzzle out so you can see them better and more easily solve the puzzle.

Much of the confusion about expressing wants occurs because no distinction is made between *wanting* and *demanding*. Stating what you want is an effort to communicate clearly, so you and your partner can both be satisfied, while demanding is insisting that your partner gives you what you want, without regard for his or her wants and feelings. Demanding is driven by a belief in scarcity and fear of not getting enough. The important difference between knowing what you want and demanding that others give it to you, or manipulating others to get it, is that knowing what you want is co-operative and contributes to successful problem solving. Demanding and manipulating is competitive and creates a struggle.

This confusion between wanting and demanding can cause us to suppress our awareness of our wants and desires, which makes it difficult, if not impossible, to satisfy them.

Your natural wanting has probably been suppressed if:

- you go blank when you try to think of what you want;
- you believe you don't care what the result is, but you feel unhappy or resentful later;
- you feel dissatisfied, but you can't put your feeling into words or think what to do about it;
- you get anxious, depressed or angry when a problem needs to be solved, because you feel you'll lose; or
- you want what everyone else wants, what you think you should want, or what someone else has, but you can't think of what you want on your own.

As adults we are responsible for satisfying our own needs and seeing to our own wants and if we don't know what we want, we'll have trouble getting it and experience a lifelong feeling of deprivation, disappointment and resentment. Feeling you can't have what you want makes it difficult to express true generosity or support for your partner to have what he or she wants. Lifelong disappointment (when you believe you cannot have what you want) stifles your enthusiasm, creativity and motivation to try to solve problems. In this way, not knowing what you want creates a false sense of scarcity and also creates competition: when there appears to be a shortage (as in a petrol shortage), people don't try to solve the problem so everyone can be satisfied (share cars, use alternative transport) but compete for the limited supply. Therefore, knowing (and saying) what you want is essential to solving problems successfully within your relationship, because only then can you work together to come up with a mutually satisfactory solution.

Even more important, often when partners state their wants they discover to their amazement that their wants are similar enough for there not to be a problem. The conflict between them was only their lack of understanding and communication. Because they didn't say what they wanted, each assumed the other wanted something different.

In the last chapter, John and Rose had set the stage for their negotiation and now it's after supper and they're settling down to talk, but neither of them has taken the time to think about what they want:

John: (taking responsibility and co-operating in the negotiation) *OK, Rose, you said you had a problem now that the children have grown-up and you felt unneeded. What do you think would help?*

Rose: (vague) *Oh, I don't know. Maybe we could do more together.*

John: (defensive) *Rose, you know that's not possible. I'm too busy at work. Be realistic.*

Rose: (feeling helpless and confused) *I'm just so depressed. I don't know what to do.*

John: (taking over) *You need to go and see a doctor, as I said before.*

Rose: (giving up) *Oh, perhaps you're right.* (end of discussion)

Both Rose and John are confused and vague, unable to discuss what they want specifically enough to reach a solution, so they end up discouraged and frustrated and less inclined to believe that negotiation will work. On the other hand, if Rose and John take the time to get clear on what they want, the discussion goes differently:

John: (taking responsibility and co-operating in the negotiation) *OK, Rose, you said you had a problem now that the children have grown-up and you felt unneeded. What do you think would help?*

Rose: (clearly stating what she wants) *Well, John, I've been thinking about it and I know I want to* *find something worthwhile to do. I enjoy taking care of people and I'm sure someone can use my skills. At the same time, I don't want to disrupt our relationship or make you unhappy. I know you're used to having me here. So, I need to find out what's most important to you about the way we've always done things.*

John: (stating his wants) *I am aware you're unhappy and I would much prefer to see you happy. But you've always been my support system and I don't want to lose that. I want to be able to phone and ask you to do something for me, or bring home business associates for dinner, or just have my usual dinner at the usual time. It really lessens my job stress to have your support.*

Rose: (considering possibilities) *That doesn't sound too difficult. If I did voluntary work or took some classes, I might not always be able to be there at the very moment you want me, but I was often out when the children had to go to the doctor or something and we always worked that out. Maybe we could work this out too.*

As Rose and John are now finding, when they remain calm and focused and clearly state their wants, it is possible, and often happens in simple negotiations, that after both of them have stated what they want, they may find that they're essentially in agreement and the problem will then easily be solved. Then the energy they would have previously expended arguing can be put into carrying out the solution to the problem.

On the other hand, if you are used to competing rather than co-operating when faced with a problem, what you and your partner want can *appear* to be so different and seem so incompatible that solving the problem will look impossible at first. But, if you persevere and complete the whole co-operative problem solving process, you will realise that discovering how different your wants are does not mean they're unsolvable.

Summarising Rose's and John's wants, the facts might look like this:

ROSE	JOHN
I want something worthwhile to do.	I want you to be a support system for me, prepare meals and entertain business associates.
I want more time for me.	I want you to be available, just as you always have.
I want to preserve our marriage.	I want to preserve our marriage.
I want you to be happy, too.	I want you to be happy, too.

Now that their wants are clearly expressed, Rose and John can understand each other. The problem is clear, which will make it easier to proceed to developing their options for solving it. The normal tendency for many people would be to worry about how far apart some of their wants seem. However, in co-operative problem solving we do not focus on this, because it would tempt us to censor our wants and make it difficult to work out and communicate what we want. The emphasis here is on what wants would have to be satisfied for you to be happy.

SKILLS IN STATING YOUR WANTS

Through understanding, you will develop the following skills:

- become aware of everything you want;
- communicate it clearly to your partner; and
- listen to your partner's wants without making assumptions, getting discouraged, jumping to conclusions or getting anxious.

In this chapter you will learn what to do if you become stuck in your negotiation and how to keep both of you motivated and hopeful about the solution. The exercises will help you explore your wants and your attitudes about wanting, in order to clear the way to having what you want, while ensuring that your partner has his or her wants satisfied too.

BARRIERS TO STATING YOUR WANTS

When you state your wants, you may be surprised to find yourself beginning to compete with each other rather than co-operate. This competitiveness can be triggered by your anxiety about the differences in your wants. In this step of the negotiation tree co-operation is important because a competitive attitude can derail your negotiation and cause you to fall back into the old habit of rescuing your mate by not stating your wants fully and clearly. Or, you may create a power struggle over who will get their way by not listening to your partner's wants.

If, when your partner is expressing what he or she wants you object to those wants, try to explain why they won't work or criticise them, you will never get a chance to fully understand what your partner's wants are. Even if you say nothing, but carry on a silent, mental commentary on what your partner wants, you will not understand them properly. Your partner has a reason to want whatever he or she wants and you must know that reason to effectively negotiate. Arguing with your partner's wants either verbally or silently makes it impossible to hear and understand your partner's position.

If you allow yourself to become afraid that your wants are too different and slide back into old power struggles or rescuing while stating and exploring your wants, you may:

- *exaggerate your want* (power struggle)   The fear that you may not get what you want may cause you to say you want more than you really do ('I want you here all the time'). You'll be reacting to the scarcity-based relief that, at best, you'll only get part of what you ask for. This is confusing to both you and your partner and because your wants are exaggerated, it looks much more difficult to reach a satisfactory solution than it really is.

- *overstate your need* (power struggle) The fear that you won't get your wants met if they are 'just wants' may cause you to state what you want as if your survival depended on it ('I'll just *die* if you don't come with me'). This causes your partner to feel suspicious that he or she is being manipulated and resist co-operating with you.
- *argue for or justify your want* (power struggle) Anxiety that your wants are not important enough to be satisfied may lead you to present them as a persuasive argument, with an overwhelming flood of reasons why you should want them or they should be satisfied ('I should get more of the money than you do, because . . .'). This can provoke your partner to object and argue in return, rather than listen.
- *not say what you want* (rescue) The belief that you won't get what you want anyway or that differences in wants will cause a fight, may lead you to say you don't care' or 'it's not important or just be silent, when the truth is you'll resent not getting what you want.
- *understate your want* (rescue) Fear that your partner will be upset, hurt or unhappy if you say what you really want may lead you to ask for something else ('I want to go to the cinema', when you really want an evening alone together) or something else. This confuses your partner and makes it impossible to solve the problem of what you really want (because you haven't said what it is).

By not clearly stating what you want, you make it impossible for your partner to clearly understand your position and, as Don and Peter discover, create competition and struggle rather than co-operation and a mutually satisfying solution.

Don and Peter have defined the problem that both of them want the back bedroom for an office and have set the stage for their negotiation, but when they try to solve the problem, they run into trouble:

Don: (stating want) *I want to use the back bedroom for my office. I'm spending too much on office space.*

Peter: (stating want, beginning to justify) *I want to use the back bedroom for my office, too, because from there I can keep an eye on Rover as he exercises in the garden.*

Don: (gets competitive) *I could always take him for a run and you could use the dining room. Besides, you only work part-time, and I work full-time, so I deserve it more.*

Peter: (getting angry, arguing) *The dining room is dark and everyone tramps through it all the time coming in and out, and I think it's about time I had a decent place to work. Besides, if you ran your business better, you'd easily be able to afford the rent on the office you already have.*

Don and Peter find themselves in an argument and no longer negotiating about what they want, because they aren't listening to each other; they're both locked in competing, trying to win. They have reverted to believing in scarcity and both assume that only one of them will get what he wants.

When Don and Peter use better communication techniques, such as 'I' messages and active listening, remember to focus on stating their own wants, listem more carefully to each other and support each other in stating their wants, the discussion has a better outcome:

Don: (stating want) *I want ot use the back bedroom for my office. My business isn't doing as well as it was and I need to cut down on my expenses.*

Peter: (active listening) *Well, I understand that you want that room for an office. It would be cheaper for you.* (stating want) *I want it too. I want to be where it's quiet and has more light, and also where I can watch the dog in the garden.*

Don: (active listening) *You want more light, less traffic and noise, and to be able to see Rover outside?*

Peter: (confirms) *Right. It sounds like our wants are clear. Is there anything you'd like to add?*

Don: *Only that it also sounds great to work here, from home.*

Peter: *It sounds good to me, too.*

Don: (ready for the next step) *OK, shall we explore our options? Let's put our heads together and see if there's a way we can both get what we want.*

Peter: *Yes. I think there's a way we can both be happy.*

Don and Peter's first attempt became competitive, because they became afraid that one of them would lose and they began arguing with each other about why one of them deserved the office more. In the second attempt, they began to co-operate, acting on the assumption that they could find a mutually satisfactory solution and trying to work together.

Using active listening and 'I' messages, they were able to stay focused on stating their wants and hearing each other, without jumping to conclusions or arguing, and therefore keep their focus on solving the problem to their *mutual* satisfaction.

To be able to work together to get both your wants satisfied, you must first state clearly what you want; to communicate what you want, you must first know what you want.

WANTING

You may be wondering why being clear about what you and your partner want is getting so much emphasis here. Many people have serious trouble knowing what they want, feeling comfortable communicating it and stating it clearly to a partner. We have found that many couples have difficulty solving problems because they do not know what they want, or, if they do know, cannot express it to a partner. If that's a problem for either or both of you, then these skills are what you need to learn to build a lasting, sustainable relationship.

In their desire to help us become more social and generous (which all small children need to learn), adults, who were also brought up to be competitive and believe in scarcity, often give us the idea (by being stressed, anxious, guilty or angry if they are not able to give us what we want) that our wants are wrong. As a result, we often grow up suppressing our desires – sometimes to the extent of not even being aware of them. As adults we carry these early childhood rules, admonitions and restrictions with us in the often unconscious form of habits, beliefs and maxims that we live by.

A child, who wants to be loved and approved of and who realises that wanting things makes Mummy or Daddy unhappy, worried, upset or angry, will eventually learn to shut the wanting off. First, you learn not to say what you want, because it upsets someone. After a few months or years, not being able to express your desires becomes too painful to endure and you learn to shut them out of your awareness.

Most of us are taught from early childhood on that our wants are selfish and that we should be polite and let others' wants come first. We are made to feel that it isn't acceptable to want ('Don't even *ask* me for a biscuit just before dinner'), or, that we can't have what we want ('*Of course* you can't have a new bike. Do you think I'm made of money?') or that, if we get what we want, someone else will be deprived (a belief in scarcity). In response, some of us learn (perhaps in competition with brothers and sisters) to grab what we can get, without considering whether we want it or not.

Even when we grow up and have the power to get most of what we want for ourselves, we continue to act on these beliefs as though we were not in charge of getting what we want. These internalised 'shoulds', 'should nots' and restrictions make us anxious about getting what we want and even convinced that we won't. This in turn leads us to compete, to rescue and to otherwise prevent ourselves from clearly knowing and stating what we want. Co-operative problem solving can help us to come up with creative and effective ways to get it.

In addition to all these other restrictions on wanting, you may have the idea that the consequences of wanting are bad (no one will like you) and so it is too frightening to know what you want. Because knowing what you want sometimes means you risk being disappointed (there may be a real reason why you can't get it) and many people have an exaggerated idea of how bad disappointment feels ('If I don't get what I want I'll be miserable'), they avoid wanting at all (thus unconsciously guaranteeing that they won't be able to get it, because you can't negotiate for a want you don't know about).

If you have any of these difficulties in being aware of what you want and communicating it to your partner, the following exercises will help you restore your natural, healthy, wanting and communicate your wants to your partner.

EXERCISE

CLARIFYING YOUR WANTS

This exercise is designed to break down the barriers that impede your awareness of what you want, to help you activate your natural ability to want and recover wants you may have suppressed since childhood.

Steps 1 and 2 are designed to help you become aware of your wants. Steps 3, 4, and 5 will deepen your understanding of these restrictions and help you know, express and communicate your true wants. Step 6 will help you overcome fears that may keep your wants suppressed and Step 7 will help you figure out what you want when all you can think of is what you don't want.

If you are doing these exercises with your partner, you can take turns reading the instructions. You will need to set aside 15 to 30 minutes at a time and in a place where you won't be interrupted. You will need a pencil and paper.

STEP 1 DISCOVERING YOUR CHILDHOOD WANTS

Read this exercise slowly, pausing where you see three dots in a row, to allow time for the fantasy to form. You may find it easier to tape record the instructions and play them back to give freedom to your imagination.

Do not stifle what you want by criticising or questioning your wants or insisting that they be logical or make sense, but allow them to come out as they are; impossible or fantastic wishes are allowed. If adult wants show up, let them, but do the best you can to stay in touch with being a child while you make your wishes.

Close your eyes, and picture youself as a young child, about seven years old . . . alone in a favourite place from your childhood . . . You might see your childhood self in your room . . . or outdoors in a special hiding place . . . where you used to go . . . Now pretend a wizard (or a magician, a genie or a fairy godmother) comes to you . . . and says you can have any wishes you can name in five minutes . . . Allow your seven-year-old self to imagine anything at all . . . What do you imagine? What do you wish for . . . ? Wish for all the material things you want . . . toys, ice-cream, new trainers, jewels, money . . . Wish for love and happiness, praise and encouragement . . . Wish for friends your own age and grown-up people who care about you . . . whatever you want.

Now, slowly, open your eyes, review what just happend in your fantasy, and write down your wants. Head your list 'My childhood wants list'.

Here's how Paul's childhood wants list looked:

MY CHILDHOOD WANTS LIST
- a boat
- cowboy boots
- plenty of time to play
- never having to go the dentist
- lots of money
- fly a plane
- be a professional footballer
- be Superman
- have a Batmobile
- lots of hugs
- a secret friend to have a tree house with

This list has some possible and impossible ideas on it, all quite natural for the seven-year-old Paul, which shows that he's in touch with his natural, childlike ability to want and able to be creative without judging and stifling what he wants. If your list sounds childlike, you are getting in touch with your natural ability to want; if your wants sound too adult ('more stability in my life', 'a better job'), repeat the exercise and spend more time on establishing your picture of a seven-year-old you.

Having experienced your childhood wants and how it feels to be in 'wanting mode', you are ready for Step 2, which will focus on your present-day, grown-up wants and help you update your want list.

STEP 2 DISCOVERING YOUR WANTS TODAY

Again, do not criticise or question your wants, just allow them to come out as they are. Allow yourself to imagine anything at all, no matter how impossible, illogical or fantastic it sounds. If an item comes up expressed in terms of 'I don't want . . .' that's allowed, too.

Now, fantasise as you did before, but this time see yourself as the adult you are today. Close your eyes, and picture yourself as you are now . . . alone in that same favourite place from your childhood . . . a special hiding place . . . where you used to go . . . Now pretend a wizard (or a magician, a genie, or a fairy godmother) comes to you . . . and says you can have any wishes you can name in five minutes . . . What do you wish for . . . ? Wish for all the material things you want . . . a sports car, a boat, win the pools, be very famous . . . and also the non-material: love and happiness, success, praise and encouragement . . . Wish for friends, people who care about you, good sex . . .

Now, slowly open your eyes, and review what just happened in your fantasy. Head your list 'My wants today' and write down your wishes.

Here's what Paul's grown-up list might look like:

MY WANTS TODAY
- £50,000 a year
- a boat
- not to work
- not to feel stressed
- not to worry about money
- no relationship worries
- cowboy boots
- a thriving business consulting and teaching
- six months off
- uninhibited sex with Michelle
- new computer with graphics
- travel – Jamaica, African safari
- play professional football
- live in village
- season tickets to football
- mountain bike
- fly my own plane

Like Paul's grown-up list, yours will probably be different from your childhood list, but contain some related things. Some of the items on your list, as on Paul's, may not seem possible (a plane, for example), but it belongs on the list anyway because it is a want.

STEP 3   OVERCOME THE BARRIERS TO WANTING

Review and contemplate both your childhood and your adult want list. As you do this, reasons why you can't have some of your wants will probably come up or thoughts that the wishes are silly, childish, greedy, not nice, selfish or wrong. You may think 'we can't afford it' or 'you don't deserve that, you haven't been good'. These internal reasons not to want are what you need to discover and counteract to release your ability to know what you want. Write down all the reasons why you think you can't have what you want in a column opposite your wants and try not to censor or argue with these negative thoughts. Just bring them into your awareness and find out what they are.

When Paul looked at his lists, his internal restrictions and objections read like this:

WHAT DO I WANT?	WHAT'S IN THE WAY?
£50,000 a year	not worth the effort can't earn that much
a boat	can't afford it

cowboy boots	won't use them enough
a thriving business consulting and teaching	can't run business by myself
six months off	can't afford it
uninhibited sex with Michelle	she'll never change
	sex dies out in long-term relationships
new computer with graphics	too much money
travel – Jamaica, African safari	too much money, no time
play professional football	too old, not enough skill
live in a village	can't earn a living
season tickets to football	too expensive
mountain bike	I'll probably get hurt
fly my own plane	don't deserve it
	can't afford it

After your list is created, evaluate how realistic your restrictions and objections are. When Paul wrote his restrictions they seemed true because he has believed them for a long time, but as he reviewed them objectively and thought about them, he realised he felt differently about them; some were obviously false ('I don't deserve it'), some were probably not true ('I'll probably get hurt'), some were actually true ('too old, not enough skill') and some were temporarily true ('I can't afford it'). Go through your own list again, and mark whether the objections are (F) false, (PF) probably false, (TT) temporarily true or (T) true. Now, in order to begin to eliminate some of your inner restrictions and open yourself to your true wants:

- when an objection is false (F), cross it out and let your want stand unobjected to;
- when an objection is probably false (PF), make a note about what you need to do to make sure it's not true (Paul wrote: get information about mountain bike safety, join a mountain bike club);
- when one is temporarily true (TT), make some notes about what you'd have to do to make it false (Paul wrote: get more education, get a better job, win the pools);
- when you find one that is true, see if you can alter the want or circumstance a bit until your objections become false. (Paul can't be a professional footballer, but he can join an amateur club.)

Paul's 'in the way' list reveals some wants that actually are impossible. 'Playing professional football' is not possible at Paul's age [Paul's objection gets a (T)] and Paul never had a professional-level skill. But, adjusting the want a little bit and joining a club in his age group is still very possible and might provide him with lots of satisfaction. Other things that he has on the list, like owning a boat, may not be possible immediately (TT), but, if he wants to put in the effort, he could buy a second-hand one or get some friends to share the cost of the boat. After research, Paul finds that season tickets to football are *not* too expensive and crosses that objection out.

In this way, Paul is able to remove some of his reasons for not wanting and open up some possibilities on his want list.

STEP 4   WHAT'S FRIGHTENING ABOUT WANTING?

You may find that when you begin to explore what you want, you feel vaguely afraid, as if it's wrong to want things too strongly or clearly. You may have old beliefs left over from childhood that say it's greedy, bad, hopeless or wrong to want things, or that bad things will happen to you, or you'll be terribly disappointed if you want them too strongly. These are not objections to individual things that you want but objections to *wanting itself*.

Write down your own ideas and fantasies about what you think are the bad things that might happen if you want too much. Keep writing things down until you feel you have captured the most frightening possible ideas on your paper. Paul's list follows as an example:

What am I afraid will happen if I want too much?
- If I get all the things I want there will probably be a catch.
- I'll want things I can't have and be disappointed and dissatisfied.
- To have all that, I'd have to be rich, and to get rich, I'd have to do things that are not nice.
- People who get everything they want mostly steal from others and don't care about others. They are not liked and they die rich and lonely.
- God will punish me if I get too greedy.
- Something bad will happen.

You can see that, with fears like these, Paul might have a difficult time allowing himself to know what he wants. However, once these fears, which are left over from childhood, are brought into awareness, they can be resolved, counteracted and reassured, so that you are free to know what you want, and therefore know how to solve your problem.

STEP 5   COUNTERACTING YOUR FEAR

Look at your list of reasons you can't have what you want. Imagine that you are encouraging and supporting a very dear friend of yours. If your friend gave you reasons (like Paul's or yours) why he or she couldn't have what he wanted and be happy, would you accept them without question and advise him or her to give up hope? Chances are, you would tell your friend that it is perfectly possible to have everything on the list and be happy, honest and well loved too. You would explain why you thought his reasons for not getting what he wants were wrong and reassure his fears by suggesting solutions for them which are encouraging and stimulate his hope, creativity and clearer thinking.

By doing two things, you can learn to reassure yourself when your objections to wanting get in the way:

1 For each fear on your list, find a solution. That is, consider what you might do:
   - solve the fearful outcome if it happens;
   - avoid it happening in the first place;
   - be more creative about finding a non-fearful way of getting what you want; or
   - reassure or rebut your dire prediction.
2 Write these solutions next to your fears.

Here's how Paul counteracted his list of fears:

WHAT IS FRIGHTENING ABOUT WANTING?	HOW TO TAKE THE FEAR OUT?
I'll want all the things I can't have and be disappointed and dissatisfied. I'll be miserable.	I can look more closely at my wants to see which ones I want enough to actually get. I can divide them into easy, medium and difficult categories. I can meet as many of my wants as I can, enjoy those and not let the others spoil my fun.
To have all those things, I'd have to be rich, and to get rich I'd have to do things that are not nice.	I can be rich, honest and fair, too. There are honest ways to make money. I could use my wealth to benefit the community. Also, I can be happy if I decide I don't want to do what I'd have to do to get things, that it isn't worth the hassle.
People who get everything they want mostly steal from others and don't care about anyone else. They are not liked and they die rich and lonely.	Not true. Many of the best things in life can't be bought with money. People are also legitimately successful in business, inherit money and are loved.

Once you have counteracted each fear, you are ready to replace it with encouragement, as in Step 6.

STEP 6   WHAT'S GOOD ABOUT WHAT I WANT?

Use each item in your solutions' list in a statement that uses it as the solution to your fears about wanting. Paul's solution looked like this:

- in order to get what I want, I must first know what I want;
- if I had lots of money, I could help my friends and others who are needy;
- wanting not to take advantage of people makes me proud;
- whether I'm rich or not, I don't want to hurt anyone;
- I can have love in my life whether or not I have money;
- I know people who know what they want, go for it and are happy;
- even if what I want seems impossible now, I can probably do it step-by-step.

You can use these positive statements to encourage yourself, and show them to your partner to use as encouragement for you (and, conversely, use your partner's positive statements when he or she needs encouragement) whenever you have difficulty giving yourself permission to want what you want.

Once you can give yourself permission to want, you may still occasionally have trouble knowing what you want, because you only know what you *don't* want. In that case, go on to Step 7.

STEP 7   GETTING FROM DON'T WANT TO DO WANT

If you're still having trouble understanding what you want, knowing what you *don't* want can help, because the opposite of anything you *don't* want can turn out to be what you *do* want. Review your *wants today* list in Step 2, and pick out anything you listed as something you *don't* want, or, if you are negotiating and can only think of what you don't want, use that.

Paul's 'don't wants' were:

- not to work;
- not to feel stressed;
- not to worry about money;
- no relationship worries.

Now take your *don't want* list and opposite each item, list the want that's implied in the 'don't want'. For example, 'I don't want to hurt any more' because 'I want to feel happy and secure'.

Here's Paul's turned around list.

not to work	BECOMES	have plenty of money
not to feel stressed	BECOMES	learn to be relaxed
not to worry about money	BECOMES	have more money, learn how to manage it better, or just worry less about it
no relationship worries	BECOMES	learn to solve problems with Michelle better, have more fun

Once you know how to turn a 'don't want' into want, you can do this anytime you or your partner are trying to solve a problem but feel confused about what you want.

However, even when you know what you want, it isn't always easy to communicate your wants clearly to your partner. You may have difficulty expressing your want because you are worried about your partner's reaction to it. Or it may be difficult for you to hear and understand your partner's wants because you're too concerned about what you want. To solve the problem co-operatively each of you needs to know what the other one wants.

COMMUNICATING WANTS

Most people who know clearly what they want but have problems expressing it to their partner, are usually using old competitive habits like:

- overstating or exaggerating wants (power struggle);
- understating wants to avoid conflict or please a partner (rescue); and
- using 'You' messages such as, 'You have to stop putting me down', instead of 'I' messages such as, 'I want to feel more respected by you' (communication skills);
- speaking from accumulated hurt and anger, which is likely to sound like blaming or complaining; such as an angry, 'I want to feel appreciated around here once in a while!' instead of a calm, 'I do a lot for our partnership and I want to know you appreciate it'; and
- being afraid to say what you want because of 'shoulds' that make you feel it's wrong.

These restrictions on saying what you want, like the restrictions on knowing what you want, confuse your partner, and this confusion distorts both of your ideas of what will solve the problem and prevents you from solving the problem to get what both of you really want.

You have already learned about most of the communication skills that overcome these problems in chapter 3. The following guidelines will help you use your new communication skills when you have a problem to solve and you need to state your wants.

GUIDELINES FOR SHARING WANTS

If you and your partner are having trouble communicating your wants, the following five steps will help you effectively take the extra time you need to make sure your wants are clear to each other, so you can understand exactly what will solve the problem and then, by continuing to follow the negotiation tree, you can find a mutually satisfactory solution.

1 *Set the stage* (chapter 4)   If the atmosphere of mutual co-operation you originally created by setting the stage has deteriorated and you are feeling frustrated, competitive or discouraged, re-create a positive atmosphere by repeating that step. Make sure you have plenty of time

and a private place, establish your good feelings about your relationship and each other, and set aside hurt and anger for the purpose of the discussion. This will make it much easier to think clearly, communicate well and hear each other, because you will begin by being calm and reassured.

2 *Use your communication skills* (chapter 3)   One of you speaks first, expressing your wants in the form of 'I' messages. Using attentive speaking to be sure your wants are being heard will make expressing your wants much more effective and efficient. The other partner will try to 'hear' all these wants, using active listening to reassure the first partner that they hear what he or she is saying. Then switch, so the first partner to speak now becomes the listener.

3 *Reassure each other* (chapter 3)   When you or your partner shows signs of needing reassurance (silent, withdraws, argues) do the following: use active listening and attentive speaking to find out your partner's fears; reassure your partner with the positive messages from Step 6 of the *clarifying your wants* exercise (page 109) or with direct answers about what you'll do if the worst happens, as in the guidelines to calm the situation down and get back to sharing your wants.

4 *Remember that you are sharing wants, not trying to resolve conflict*   Here, your only task is to understand what your partner wants and communicate what you want. Questioning whether a want is OK, arguing with or criticising what your partner wants, or suggesting solutions, is premature and will create defensiveness and competitiveness between you. Working out any differences you have comes in a later step in the negotiation tree.

5 *Say exactly what you want, not more, not less*   Monitor what you say to be sure you are not using any of the barriers to wanting (exaggerating, understating, overstating, justifying or arguing, or not stating your wants) to avoid or manipulate your partner's response. If you find that you're using a barrier, or you get confused about what you want, go back to the *clarifying wants* exercise and review them, then come back to your partner and re-state them as clearly and calmly as you can.

As you become more adept at stating your wants, you'll find that because you care about each other's wants, it's easier to maintain an attitude of co-operation and avoid struggling or competing. Knowing what you want, being able to communicate it clearly with your partner and turning your 'don't wants' into wants helps each of you to be better understood and makes it easier for both of you to work together to get *both* your wants met. This frees you to move on to the final steps of the negotiation tree – *exploring options and deciding* – which will show you how to fulfil both your own and your partner's wants.

CHAPTER 6

EXPLORE YOUR OPTIONS AND DECIDE

In the previous chapter, you and your partner learned to identify and communicate what you want. Once you both understand your wants clearly you will discover one of three things:

1 Your wants are so similar or compatible that the solution is obvious and the problem is solved. It was merely your lack of understanding, miscommunication or lack of awareness of what both of you wanted that made it look as if there was a problem. When that happens, it's not necessary to explore options, because the problem is already solved for you, like John and Rose's problem in the last chapter. If clarifying your wants has led you to believe that your problem is virtually solved, you can turn directly to the section called *deciding and confirming your decision* (page 131).

2 Your wants seem compatible but you haven't come to a definite solution. In this case, you will feel reassured by knowing what you both want and proceed to creatively explore new options (*brainstorm*) and discuss them until the solution becomes clear.

   When Carol and Paul clarified their wants about housework, they found that both of them wanted someone else to do it, which left them with clear, compatible wants but no solution as yet.

3 Your wants seem in conflict or appear to be unsolvable. Often, although your wants are clear and you both understand them, if there is a conflict in the wants you have expressed, a mutually satisfactory solution isn't obvious:

   Paul might want a beach holiday (to swim and relax in the sun) while Mary wants to go to the mountains (to walk and get exercise and clean air).

   Fred might want sex three times a week and Naomi might prefer it once every two weeks.

   Don and Peter might struggle over what seems like not enough space in the house for both of them to have their offices there.

When your wants seem to be in such conflict, finding a mutually satisfactory solution is more difficult than when they are compatible, but not impossible. In this chapter, you will learn to find a workable, mutually satisfying solution without allowing your anxiety about differing wants to activate old competitive methods of problem solving, such as power plays and rescues.

Explore your options and decide is the part of the negotiation tree that most of us think of as the problem solving part of solving a problem – developing possible solutions, determining the best and making a decision.

Because in the previous steps you have done all the work of creating an atmosphere of co-operation, mutual caring and clear communication, explore your options and decide is usually the most fun and the easiest step of all. Now you and your partner are able to play with ideas, to consider both fantastic and practical options and to pool your creative energy by brainstorming. This creative approach to the problem will allow you to develop ideas and options you would not have thought of before. These will break your stalemate and help you find a way to solve the problem so that both your wants are satisfied. In the rare case that you are still stuck with unresolved differences after brainstorming, you will learn how to experiment and explore new possibilities to see if they might work. Whether your problem is simple, like who does what around the house, or complex, such as solving sexual problems or working out money worries, following the guidelines and techniques in this chapter will lead you to success.

SKILLS AND BARRIERS IN EXPLORING OPTIONS

This means thinking of as many possible solutions to choose from as you can. The more choices you have, the more likely it is that a mutually satisfactory solution can be found. The skills you will learn to facilitate exploring options and deciding are:

- the *abundance worksheet*, which helps you overcome the fear that your problem cannot be solved by teaching you how to gain a deeper understanding of the dynamics underlying the problem and look at it from a new, more creative perspective;
- *brainstorming*, in which you creatively think of new options until you have enough to solve the problem;
- *research and experimenting*, which helps you gather more information when you can't work out a mutually satisfactory solution;
- *deciding*, a simple process of picking the best option out of several;
- *confirming the decision*, which ensures you have not overlooked any confusion or misunderstanding in your choice;
- *celebration*, which acknowledges and confirms your successful decision and creates confidence in your ability to solve problems and enthusiasm for the next negotiation; and
- *renegotiation*, which takes the pressure off your decision making by allowing you to accommodate unexpected life changes.

The barriers that are likely to get in the way of exploring options and deciding are:

- *apparent scarcity*: feeling anxious that the problem is unsolvable, which can tempt you to compete, power-play or rescue, thus preventing you from finding a co-operative solution;
- *hopelessness*: becoming overwhelmed by trying to solve all possible aspects, past, present and future (which are usually unforeseeable) of the problem now, which discourages both of you and makes creative thinking difficult;
- *confusion*: misunderstanding or mistaking your agreement, which leads to thinking you have the problem solved when you don't;
- *criticism*: stifling brainstorming by being critical of suggested ideas, which prevents you from freely suggesting new options and limits the possible solutions to the problem.

If you are caught up in any of the above barriers, you may not see all the possible options (and therefore, not be able to make the best choice) because your anxiety about your differences will interfere with your creative thinking. In most cases it is actually only the *perception* of the people involved that no possible mutually satisfactory solution can be found, or that someone's wants will have to go unsatisfied, or that the problem is impossible to solve. If you do get stuck in what seems to be an impossible problem, instead of letting your fears push you into competing and arguing, you can recognise that it is just an *apparent scarcity*, and use the abundance worksheet in this chapter to examine your deeper wants and expand your boundaries to end the stalemate. You will probably find that there are plenty of workable options and a mutually beneficial solution can be found.

Don and Peter used the abundance worksheet to break their power struggle and find out what lay behind each of their wants for an office, so each of them could understand the other better, feel less afraid of being unsatisfied and work together to find a mutual solution.

Hopelessness can be overcome by a *research project or experiment*. If even the abundance worksheet doesn't help and you feel that you will never find a way to solve your problem, you probably don't have enough information, so setting up a research project to gather more facts or an experiment to see which possible solutions might work, will reassure you that a solution is possible and give you the extra knowledge you need to find one. When Paul wasn't sure that having a cleaner would work for him, he and Carol experimented with a housecleaning service on a trial basis before making their final decision.

Even after you've reached a decision, it's possible for one or both of you to be confused or to differ in your understanding of what the decision is, so *confirming the decision* is a skill that helps you verify that you both know what solution you've agreed to. Paul and Carol found that confirming their decision by writing it down eliminated their confusion.

Finally, even the best of solutions may not be workable forever, because situations and people change, so *renegotiation* will help you be flexible and able to adapt to change, and make finding a workable solution less overwhelming. Being able to renegotiate at any time means you don't have to be able to predict what might happen in the future in order to reach a decision today, because you can renegotiate if the situation changes.

Once you've reached a successful decision, *celebrating* your success helps you acknowledge what you have accomplished, put a clear and positive end to the negotiation, increase your warmth and goodwill and reward yourselves for work well done.

When you have explored options through the abundance worksheet and brainstorming, made your decision, confirmed it and celebrated, your co-operative negotiation is complete, and you and your partner will have the satisfaction of successful teamwork, mutual support and a mutually satisfying result.

BRAINSTORMING

Once it is clear what each of you want, if the solution isn't obvious, you must find a way to come up with ideas that have not occurred to you before, until you find one or more that will solve the problem to your satisfaction. But developing new options can be difficult unless you can break the habitual thinking processes that can block creativity:

- *rigid or limited ideas* ('shoulds') that say you can only do things in certain, pre-set ways (such as the way your family did it) and prevent you from considering new options that may suit you better;
- *criticism* which can stifle new ideas by attacking them for not being perfect before they are even fully formed; and
- *old, ingrained thinking habits* which can prevent you from seeing possible solutions because you have never considered them before.

If you're having difficulty developing an option that will solve the problem so that both of you are satisfied, you can stir your creative imagination by learning to *brainstorm*. Brainstorming was created to overcome limitations on creativity and it will help you and your partner free your thinking and explore options. It will also help you decide if you need further information and, when it is necessary, to set up a research project.

Your creativity is limited when you:

- see a problem only one way;
- are so accustomed to a particular way of doing things that other ideas don't occur to you;
- approach problem solving with a perfectionistic, hopeless or critical attitude;
- have been taught by your family or society that an option is unthinkable; and
- don't have enough information.

Learning to brainstorm shows you how to overcome criticism and its blockage of your creative ideas by getting playful and energetic and allowing even silly or impossible ideas to be part of the process. By not considering the reasonableness of options until after brainstorming, you give your creativity free reign. To brainstorm, you think of and make a list of all kinds of ideas for solving the problem, as many as you possibly can, as quickly as you can. It is important to write down every idea, whether or not it seems to make sense, be possible, or be reasonable. If you eliminate ideas because they are not reasonable, practical, sensible or acceptable at this point, you will block the flow of new ideas and stifle your creativity. Brainstorming breaks through old familiar concepts and stimulates new, more creative ideas by creating conditions that encourage a non-critical, unrestricted, free flow of ideas.

In brainstorming, you and your partner learn to freely generate ideas you haven't thought of before, write them down, review them, evaluate them and choose the best solution. The point of brainstorming is to break through the limits of your previous thinking by getting outrageous, silly, creative and inventive. Through this energetic, fun process, you will be able to find innovative solutions to seemingly unsolvable problems.

You will know that your thinking is not restricted when you have as many silly ideas as usable ones. When your thinking *is* restricted, the exercise will show you how to loosen it up. The intention of brainstorming is to generate new ideas and remove the limitatons that normally would inhibit the flow.

EXERCISE

BRAINSTORMING

Choose a place where you won't be interrupted and allow 20 to 45 minutes, depending on the difficulty of the problem. Have a large pad and pens or markers for writing down your ideas because physically moving around helps you to stay loose and energised.

1   WRITE THE PROBLEM DOWN

Write down the problem in terms of each of your basic wants so that it is in sight while you brainstorm. It's the reason why you are trying to generate the options and having it in front of you will be a constant reminder to help you stay on track. If you have trouble, follow the steps in the your *discovering your wants today exercise* (chapter 5, page 110).

2   WRITE AS MANY IDEAS AS YOU CAN IN TEN MINUTES

We recommend that you each write your ideas on the pad as you come up with them, to keep you moving and raise the energy level. Set a timer for ten minutes. During that time, each of you should try to contribute as many ideas as you can, calling them out and writing them down. Saying your ideas out loud as well as writing them creates a playful atmosphere, reminiscent of a game of charades or a television game show. Be silly, be boisterous, shout ideas out, don't worry about being sensible or reasonable, get as excited as a game-show contestant does. Remember, the first ideas may be hesitant, but as you begin to toss ideas back and forth, your energy will rise. The more your energy flows, the more your ideas will flow. Don't criticise or comment on the ideas. You can evaluate each other's ideas later.

3   WHEN YOUR TEN MINUTES ARE UP, REVIEW YOUR LIST

Enjoy the wild or silly suggestions. Each of you underline the ones that work for you. If there are options that you both like, pick the one you agree is best and proceed to clarify and confirm your decision as discussed on page 131

4   IF THERE IS NO IDEA THAT'S GOOD ENOUGH FOLLOW STEPS 1–3 AGAIN

You may need to do several ten-minute brainstorming sessions to get the creativity flowing and reach a solution that works for both of you. Remember, the more fun you have, the more creative you'll be, but do try to stay focused on addressing the problem.

APPARENT SCARCITY

If you or your partner are still having trouble stating and exploring wants, the problem may be an *apparent scarcity*. One or both of you may have become caught up in the perception that there is no possible solution because there isn't enough of something (time, money, love, patience, food, goodwill, space, energy) to go around so that both of you can get what you want. This is an 'apparent' scarcity because the scarcity only *appears* real. The vast majority of scarcities are not real, because what appears to be a scarcity is usually created by competition and almost always disappears when carefully examined in terms of what the partners really want. Because most people's first response is to compete, couples are often convinced that there is a scarcity (someone's going to be dissatisfied) before they even see whether at least one satisfactory solution can be found.

When we fear that we will not get our wants and needs met, our natural reaction is to defend our 'share' and compete for what we want. When this happens, it will make us less able to hear our partner's wants, or to state our own calmly and without exaggeration. This competition can create the very scarcity we fear by blinding us to all the options that are available, as it did with Don and Peter. Then anxiety prevented them from seeing any options in their first discussion but they came up with many when they conquered their fear of scarcity and tried brainstorming.

OVERCOMING APPARENT SCARCITY

The perception of scarcity arises from false limits – a belief that you can't both have what you want prevents you from considering all the possibilities – placed on the problem. Creating abundance depends on expanding these limits. This can be done in two ways:

1 *Examine your wants* Often, we come up with an instant idea of what we want, without stopping to think about why we want it or whether it will really satisfy us. Often this idea, stated as a want, is, in fact, a possible solution that might satisfy a want, rather than the want itself.

For Don, using the back bedroom for his office was his *solution* for saving on rent and feeling isolated and alone in his office. His *actual* underlying wants were to save money and have some company, but he passed over them and came up with a possible solution, which he presented to Peter as his want. To Peter it felt like a decision which had already been made, limiting Peter's options.

If your wants are in conflict with your partner's and you can't find an option that will satisfy you both, take time to examine exactly what you want, why you want it and if there are any other options that can help you break through some of the limits and make it much easier to reach a mutually satisfying solution.

2 *Expand your boundaries* Expanding your boundaries means becoming aware of artificial limitations (false ideas or family and cultural taboos that you shouldn't or can't do something) that keep you from considering options that would resolve your apparent scarcity.

Don had settled on the back bedroom as the only solution but when he realised he was limiting his options, he discovered many possibilities (saving to extend the house, sharing a rented office suite, renting a caravan and parking it in the driveway, making the dining room into his office so Peter could use the back bedroom, or converting part of the garage).

Naomi and Fred, who are having sexual problems, believe there is scarcity in their relationship. Fred is dissatisfied with the frequency and availability of sexual relations with Naomi and Naomi feels a lack of cuddling and affection. When they explored their options, Fred discovered that paying a little extra affectionate attention (hand holding, hugging, casual touching during the day, sitting close while watching TV) to Naomi got her interested in being sexual with him much more often, and Naomi discovered that when she wasn't feeling as sexual as Fred, he was satisfied with masturbating while she held him, or watching erotic films together, as long as she was happy, too.

Often there appears to be a lack of options because you are only looking in one place or at one moment for the solution to your problem. We found, when doing this exercise in workshops, that if we gave a group of ten people three or four grapes and told them 'there is enough to go around' they tended to focus on how ten people might share four grapes, never noticing that there were several pounds of grapes close by. Even though we said nothing about being limited to the grapes we handed them, they automatically limited their boundaries to what they were given. Most of them said they 'didn't think to look around' or 'thought they shouldn't ask for more grapes', although there were no such rules.

In a similar way, although neither Paul nor Carol want to do housework, they don't consider bringing in a cleaning service to do it, so they have an apparent scarcity (of someone who is willing to do it). Similarly, you or your partner may think you have to have a solution immediately when you actually have a few days or weeks, and in that extra time, you can easily find a mutually satisfactory option.

If, after you and your partner have stated your wants, you have tried generating options but you still don't believe you can both get what you want, the following exercise will help you break out of limited thinking, expand your boundaries and discover new options so you can stay focused on co-operative problem solving rather than letting the apparent scarcity draw you into competing.

While you will find it is easier to think of options for some problems than for others, any time you feel that the problem is unsolvable or feel helpless or hopeless about it, you may be facing an apparent scarcity. Using the *abundance worksheet* will show you that a solution is probably possible, and you will feel reassured, more hopeful and able to think more clearly.

EXERCISE

THE ABUNDANCE WORKSHEET

The *abundance worksheet* is a tool for you and your partner to use to get you moving again when you can't find options to solve an apparent scarcity due to a conflict between your wants. Follow the instructions below.

We've shown you how Don and Peter did each step as an example to follow.

STEP 1   DESCRIBE THE APPARENT SCARCITY

The purpose of this step is to summarise the problem. List both partners' wants, arguments, explanations, and rationalisations of why you want what you want and the limits you believe you will encounter. Then, pare down your original description until you can develop a summary sentence or two that states what the problem appears to be:

Peter wants back bedroom for office. Don wants it, too. Limited rooms available. Eliminate travel time and expense to work, wear on car. Save cost of office rent. Amount of space needed. We both need offices.

Summary: We both want the back bedroom for an office and there's not enough room for both of us.

STEP 2   EXPLORE WANTS

The purpose of this step is to delve more deeply into what you want and to try and discover the wants behind your stated wants. It's OK to include what you don't want, because as you have seen in the previous exercise, you can turn your 'don't wants' around and they become wants. Do this by asking yourself the following questions:

- Why do I want what I've stated as my wants?
- What would accomplishing my wants change or solve for me?
- What about the current situation makes me dissatisfied or unhappy and how will getting what I want solve it?

Once you have answered these questions, you'll be able to write a list of what you want, ending with your ideal option, like Don and Peter:

DON'S WANTS

I want the back bedroom for an office because:

I need to reduce my overheads.

I hate commuting.

I don't like being isolated at my current office.

I want equal rights and equal opportunities in this relationship. It's my house, too.

Ideally: My option would be: money to have an office suite near home to share with others.

PETER'S WANTS

I want the back bedroom for an office because:

I want a light room to work in (dining room is too dark).

I want to be able watch my dog in the back garden.

I don't want to pay extra rent for an office.

Ideally: My option would be to work at home to be with Rover, and the back bedroom would make the best office.

Continue asking yourself the questions and expanding your lists, until you feel you have got down to your most basic wants and options about the issue. Then share your lists. As you explore your underlying, more detailed wants, enough new options should become clear to you so that your apparent scarcity disappears and you can go on to exploring options and deciding.

Don and Peter learned a lot about themselves and each other by exploring what they wanted and the problems became less threatening because they could see the reasons behind the wants and understand each other's position better. But they didn't feel that the apparent scarcity was completely gone. If exploring wants does not give you enough information, go on to the next step.

STEP 3   EXPAND THE BOUNDARIES OF THE PROBLEM

The purpose of this step is to help you remove any arbitrary and previously unnoticed restrictions or false limits you and your partner may have placed on the possible solutions to your problem. Answer the following questions as they relate to your apparent scarcity:

- Is there anything you have not considered doing, having, saying or trying because you don't think it's worth mentioning?
- How can you stretch your view of what's possible and what your resources are?
- Can you include more space, more time, other people or money you weren't thinking of before?
- Are there any 'shoulds' you don't really need to obey?
- What are the limitations you are placing on the situation?

For Don and Peter, looking beyond the boundaries produced the following options:

- Use the dining room.
- Convert the garage.
- Use the attic or the basement.
- Add a room.
- Get a caravan in the drive.
- Move to a larger house.
- Rent space nearby.
- Reorganise the house, move the bedroom into the dining room, eat in the kitchen and use both bedrooms for office space.
- Both squeeze into the back bedroom and pay Don's office rent into a building fund.
- Whoever gets the bedroom shares the cost for the other to rent an office outside.

In exploring their wants and expanding their boundaries, the partners learned a lot about each other and themselves and can now see that a solution is not as impossible as they previously thought. Don and Peter have so many new and promising options that their problem should be quite easy to solve now.

Fred and Naomi's problem, being intangible and emotional, and involving sex – an issue which is difficult for many people to talk frankly about – could be more difficult to solve than Don and Peter's more mundane and concrete issue. But when they explored their wants and expanded their boundaries, they came up with the following ideas:

- Sex doesn't always have to be the same for both of us. Fred could masturbate and Naomi could just hold him as he does.
- We could cuddle and watch erotic films, so Fred can feel sexy and Naomi can get affection.
- Affection can include holding hands, talking quietly, sending flowers.
- Naomi can ask Fred for whatever would make her feel safe whenever he makes a sexual overture.

- Fred and Naomi could go for marital therapy and find out more options.

After expanding your boundaries and exploring options, you may discover that you still have doubts or questions that indicate that you don't have enough information to really solve the problem (what are the legal issues? how will it feel to do something new? can we really live up to our agreement?). If this is the case, then setting up a research project will help you find the answers.

DOING RESEARCH

Usually, when you have found an option you both like, it is easy to move forward to a decision to implement it to solve your problem. There are times, however, when an immediate solution isn't obvious, because more information is needed. Sometimes one or both of you may not be certain about whether or not the option you have selected is the right one. For example:

- you may come up with a good idea, but you don't know if it will really work until you gather more facts;
- you may come up with an idea that you think will work, but you won't know until you try it;
- one partner may be delighted with an idea, but the other won't be sure until he or she sees what it's really like.

When this happens, you need to research either by gathering information or trying out your solution on a temporary basis.

EXPERIMENTATION: TRY IT OUT TEMPORARILY

The only way to find out if some solutions (such as who does a particular household chore, how to handle a problem with your families the next time it comes up, a new sexual variation or changing the layout of your living room) will work is to try them on an experimental basis. If you and your partner find yourself in a situation where you think you have a solution but you're not sure if it will work, or one of you is worried that you'll be unhappy with it, trying it out on an experimental basis allows you to see whether or not it actually works before making a decision. By not testing a possible solution, you will not have the benefit of the information you will gather from a trial run. By agreeing to try a solution for a period of time, you can find out if it actually works and if it is mutually satisfactory.

The guidelines for doing research (page 129) will show you how.

The second type of research you may need to do in order to have enough information to decide on a mutually satisfactory solution is *gathering information.*

GATHERING INFORMATION

*I*f, when you have considered options, you find you have a lot of unanswered questions (how much will it cost? how long will it take? do we know enough to do it ourselves, or should we hire someone?) and need more facts before you'll know if a proposed solution is feasible, you can research by gathering information.

Gathering information means checking with resources (look it up in the library, take a class or workshop, call businesses in the yellow pages, ask a lawyer, a doctor, a therapist, a plumber, a travel agent, a mechanic or other expert, or ask friends or business associates who have tried whatever you want to know about and have more information than you do about what you need to know.

When you agree to do information research, just as in the trial solution research, it is important to set a time to get back together and share what you've learned, to see if your chosen option is indeed feasible.

In the rare cases when brainstorming and the abundance worksheet don't lead to a solution, it is possible that there actually is not an immediate or obvious solution available that will satisy both of you. Sometimes you and your partner may be uncertain whether the options you've considered are possible because you don't possess all the knowledge you need to evaluate them. If that is the case, you will want to initiate a formal research project, as in the following guidelines:

GUIDELINES FOR DOING RESEARCH

Once you have a possible solution, but you have questions about how it will work, agree to research in the same way you reached an agreement to negotiate.

It is usually easier to get an agreement if you both restate that the purpose of the research is to get more information that will help both of you get your wants met.

If one partner does not agree that research is a good idea at this point, use your communication skills to find out why. If the reluctant partner is worried about something, use reassurance to answer what you would do if that negative something happens. If the reluctance is due to something else, then treat it as a new problem to be negotiated.

Decide whether the type of research you do will be:

A *Experimentation* (trying a solution for a limited period of time to see how it works, as Paul and Carol did when they hired a housekeeper on a trial basis for a month). To experiment, pick one of your possible solutions to try out.

B *Information gathering* (seeking out more facts and details about the solution until you know how it works). Paul and Mary found out more about travelling by splitting the work: Paul telephones travel agents to see what resorts that have mountains and lakes with beaches are available and Mary goes to the library to look at travel magazines and books on holiday ideas.

They talk to friends and read the travel advertisements in the Sunday papers together.

Once you have agreed on the research, follow the guidelines below, depending on whether you've decided to experiment or to gather more information.

GUIDELINES FOR EXPERIMENTING

1 *Set a time limit*   Decide how long you'll try your experiment (Carol and Paul decided on one month) before you get back together and discuss the results. (This is a rough estimate. In the next step you will actually set a time and place to resume your negotiation, after experimenting.) Limiting the time for the trial will reassure both of you that you haven't yet committed yourself to a decision you're not sure of and it will also ensure you don't forget to complete the negotiation.

2 *Set a time and place*   Set another meeting date when you can discuss how the trial went and whether the solution works or not. This provides the uninterrupted, unhurried time you need to discuss the results of your experiment and complete your negotiation.

3 *Conduct the experiment*   Try your temporary solution for the specified time, with both of you paying attention to how well you think it works. This trial period will give you the experience you need to know if your solution is mutually satisfying. You may want to make notes to use in your discussion later, to ensure that you will be able to communicate the results of your experiment, how well you liked or didn't like it, and what you learned from it to each other.

Paul and Carol met after the cleaner had been there several times, and Paul decided the cleaning solution was fine with him – no privacy problem, because he wasn't home at that time. Carol loved the extra help and was less tired after work. She was more pleasant and they both decided the expense was well worth it, so they agreed that their problem was solved. If the trial had not solved their problem, they would have resumed brainstorming, using the new information they had from having tried the cleaner.

4 *Resume negotiation*   After the trial period, meet at the specified time and place and discuss the information you gained from your experiment. If your trial experiment seems to satisfy both of you, your problem is solved. If it doesn't work, resume exploring options and continue on through the negotiation tree.

GUIDELINES FOR GATHERING INFORMATION

1 *Divide work*   Decide what information you need and where it is available and divide up the work. One of you contacts half of the sources, the other contacts the rest. If your work is near the library, for example, it makes sense for you to get the library information.

2 *Set time and place*   Set another meeting date when you can discuss the information you've

gathered and how it changes your ideas and your opinions of the possible solutions. This will ensure that you resume negotiation when you've gathered all the facts and also puts a time limit on how long you have to complete your research.

3 *Gather information* Do whatever research you agreed on, take notes, gather pamphlets, articles, facts and figures as needed and summarise what you've found out so that you can explain it to your partner.

4 *Resume negotiation* Meet at the specified time and place to discuss the information you've gathered. The new facts you've gathered will probably make it clear which option will satisfy both of you and your problem will be solved. If not, you may want to try an experiment or return to exploring options.

DECIDING AND CONFIRMING YOUR DECISION

Once you have come up with a solution you can both agree on, it may seem that because you have found an acceptable option, your negotiation has been successful and the process is complete.

However, it is still possible that if you end the process here, you might unwittingly create three problems:

1 One of you may not really be in full agreement because you realise the agreement places some undue burden on you, but you haven't expressed your reservations. This is our old friend, the rescue, coming up one last time and causing you to not want to disappoint the partner who is excited about the option. As always, rescuing builds resentment, and you could find that the agreement you thought you had made doesn't really work.

When Don and Peter discussed their new office situation, Don noticed he felt a little burdened and resentful but he didn't say anything, because their negotiation had taken quite a long time and he thought Peter might be upset if he objected. So, when the time came to move the offices, Don felt angry and was irritable and uncooperative.

2 You and your partner may understand the agreement differently and not realise it because you haven't restated it clearly. Inadvertently you have created different hidden expectations that will erupt later.

When Paul and Carol decided to try a cleaner they created some confusion:

Paul: *Right, here's the agreement: We pay for a cleaner for a one month trial period. We'll see if we can* *get someone for £40 a day. Then we'll meet the first Saturday after the month is up and decide if we like the arrangement.*

Carol: *Good. I'll look for a cleaner.*

Carol did find one who charged £40 a day and agreed to work every Wednesday for one month. It wasn't until the fourth cleaning day that Paul realised she was coming weekly, when he thought she was going to come twice a month. He was dismayed to discover his cost was twice what he thought it was.

3 You may not both feel equally satisfied and not realise it, because you haven't been clear about what is expected from each of you and what each of you expects to get from the agreement, which can lead to one partner unconsciously sabotaging or not keeping to the agreement.

Paul got really enthused about their holiday in the mountains, and decided on a resort. Mary agreed at first but later began to realise that the resort wasn't nearly as luxurious as she wanted and she started complaining about something every time Paul mentioned the trip: the packing was difficult, the airline food would be lousy, who would care for the cat while they were away. Mary's disappointment was causing her to unconsciously sabotage their plans.

To avoid these problems, you must be certain that you are both in agreement about the solution, that you and your partner understand your agreement in the same way and that you are both equally satisfied. To ensure this, you will need to formally decide on a solution, confirm and then finalise your decision.

DECIDING

*I*f you have done the proper groundwork by exploring options until you have several good ones to choose from, brainstorming if you don't have enough and experimenting or gathering information if you need more facts, deciding is usually very straightforward. Once you have enough possible solutions for the problem, at least one acceptable one will stand out to each of you. If you have not done enough preliminary work, you will not have enough options or one or both of you will feel dissatisfied with what you have. In this case, you need to go back and repeat an earlier step: the abundance worksheet, brainstorming, or a research project. In rare cases, one partner will simply be unwilling to make a decision. In that case, you need to solve the problem for yourself, as in the guidelines in chapter 3 (page 84).

When you have selected a mutually satisfying decision, you will feel a sense of achievement or relief. When a problem is solved, the tension involved in recognising that your wants are different and that you are not yet satisfied, relaxes.

When Paul and Carol had completed their decision about housework, Carol noticed a feeling of relief, a relaxation of tension, when she thought she wouldn't have to deal with housecleaning and she had Paul's support and approval for the solution. Paul felt relieved, too. Without realising it, he had felt pressured and guilty about not wanting to do his share. Being co-operative, honest about their wants and successful at finding a viable, mutually satisfying solution was gratifying and they both felt full of goodwill and celebration. If you feel relieved, enthusiastic or satisfied when you have come to your decision, you are ready to finalise your agreement.

Here are simple guidelines for making a decision, once you have enough options.

GUIDELINES FOR DECIDING

1 *Choose your individual favourite*   From the options that you've developed on your abundance worksheet, through the brainstorming exercise or through a research project, each of you choose separately the option or options you feel satisfies your wants. If you really do not have an option that satisfies you, do the brainstorming exercise again, or begin a research project to get more information. When you can select a favourite option, go to Step 2.

2 *Share your choices*   Tell each other what your favourite choice is. If you've chosen the same one, your decision is made and you can go on to confirming your decision. If you choose different options, go on to Step 3.

3 *Try to combine choices*   Look for a way to combine your favourite choices into one option that covers both of them. You can use your brainstorming techniques or the abundance worksheet to generate the new, combined idea. Once Paul and Mary agreed on a mountain resort by a lake, Paul wanted a simple resort but Mary's choice was a more luxurious one. They found out they could combine choices by choosing a resort in a country park that had all the amenities of a fine hotel, including a lake and a pool, but had walking and fishing also available. When you believe you have found a suitable combination, move on to Step 4.

4 *Check for relief*   Check with each other to see how you feel about the decision. Once your decision is made, you should both feel somewhat relieved, relaxed and satisfied. If you do, your decision is made and you can go on to confirming the decision. If you don't feel relieved or satisfied about your decision, mentally review your response to the proposed solution. Does something feel ignored or unfinished? Do you seem to have vague objections or doubts about it? If so, your decision is still not complete and you need to brainstorm. Use the abundance worksheet, or set up a research project to generate more information.

When Don and Peter discussed their new office situation, Don noticed he felt a little burdened and resentful and he realised their decision meant he was agreeing to a lot of work and responsibility so that he could have a new outside office. He discussed his reservations with Peter. As a result, they modified their decision to give Peter more of the responsibility for the work. At that point, the agreement felt much more equal to Don, and he felt relieved and happy to make the decision. Peter still felt he was getting what he wanted and was happy to make the adjustment.

If, like Don, you feel uneasy, confused or unsure, you may:

- discuss your misgivings with your partner;
- review the decision for flaws or omissions, and go back to brainstorming to develop more options or fine tune the ones you have;
- decide to experiment with your decision to see if it works well. If you are experiencing some doubt and cannot work out what it is, turn your best options into an experiment, using the guidelines for doing research.

CONFIRMING THE DECISION

Once an option has been selected and agreed upon, to be sure both of you attribute the same interpretation to your solution and that you both understand and agree to the same decision, it is still necessary to make a formal agreement confirming your choice. To *confirm your decision*, each of you reviews the decision in your own mind and communicates your understanding of it to the other in enough detail to be sure that you are both agreeing to the same decision. Skipping this important step could lead you to creating a hidden expectation on both your parts. You may find out later on that each of you understood the agreement differently. One of you could be diligently carrying out your part of the supposed agreement only to discover that the other partner has different expectations of what you would do and is furious with you for not keeping your word, as when Paul was dismayed to find out that they were paying for twice as much cleaning time as he thought.

To confirm your decision, follow these guidelines:

GUIDELINES FOR CONFIRMING YOUR DECISION

In your own words, express your understanding of the decision you have reached. This is a verbal run-through or practice of your agreement, which allows you to make sure you've covered all the details and gives you a chance to imagine together how satisfactory your solution will be. Each of you should share:

- your understanding of what the solution is and how it will work. (When Paul and Carol reconfirmed their decision about housework to clear up the confusion, Paul said, 'As I understand it, we'll hire the cleaner to come every other week and we'll split the cost'. Carol agreed.);
- what you expect to contribute to the solution (Paul and Carol would each pay half the cost); and
- how you will benefit from the solution (Paul and Carol both get a clean house, Carol will be less stressed and Paul won't have to do housework).

FINALISING YOUR AGREEMENT

Once you both have confirmed your decision, make a formal agreement, like a contract. When co-operative problem solving is new to you or when your decision is complex, we recommend you avoid possible disagreement or unhappiness later by writing a formal agreement that lists what you both feel you have decided on. Verbal agreements can leave room for misunderstandings like Paul and Carol's because you may skip over important details. Writing down your agreement minimises these problems by revealing any obvious areas of misunderstanding about your decision and by forcing you to be clearer and more precise about the specifics of your agreement. This ensures that you both understand exactly what the agreement is, and if you get confused later, you can check your written agreement to clear up the confusion.

Because they settled for a verbal agreement last time, Paul and Carol created confusion, so this time they decided to write out their contract. Carefully written out, Paul and Carol's new contract read, 'We will hire the cleaner to come one day, every other week, for a one-month trial period, at a cost of no more than £40 each time'.

Once you become familiar with co-operative problem solving you will usually find it sufficient to confirm your decision verbally, in a few words informally stated. But when a problem is complex or long standing, a written contract is always helpful in making sure your agreement is clear.

Read your written agreement out loud and let each other know you've agreed to it. Once you've done this, your agreement is finalised, unless circumstances change, requiring a change in your solution. If Don were offered an excellent job, he might give up his business, making an office unnecessary, or if someone fell ill in Mary's family, and she and Paul decided to use their holiday to help out, their plans would be shelved. For that reason, in co-operative problem solving you need to note as part of your agreement that all solutions will be renegotiable at any time.

RENEGOTIATION

In order to honour your commitment to each other's satisfaction, any solution must be renegotiable if either of you becomes unhappy with it. No couple can foresee all possible events and any solution that works in the situation you have today may be obsolete when something different happens tomorrow. As you grow older, like Rose and John, your external circumstances may change (retirement, grown-up children, new interests), or you may become more successful, or problems may arise, or you may just grow tired of the way you are doing things. Co-operating means working together to find new solutions if old solutions no longer work for one or both of you.

Because none of us can predict the future, it is impossible to find solutions that will cover all these eventualities. Trying to find the perfect solution that will do this can create pressure and anxiety and make a solution seem impossible, which can in turn bring back old competitive behaviour.

GUIDELINES FOR SUCCESSFUL RENEGOTIATION

1 Begin by adding the phrase 'all solutions are renegotiable at any time' to all your agreements. This removes the pressure to make the solution perfect for all possible outcomes and reassures both of you that you can always renegotiate.

2 Renegotiate your agreements instead of breaking or deviating from them. If you can break an agreement any time it becomes inconvenient or unpleasant for you, your partner will never be able to trust your agreements, and vice versa. Renegotiating makes sure no one is surprised, betrayed or deceived, and enhances the trust between you.

3 Just as you did in agreeing to negotiate, let your partner know that your previous solution isn't working for you, and why, and formally request a renegotiation.

4 If an emergency occurs and you are forced to break an agreement without renegotiating, formally acknowledge that you did it, explain why it was an emergency and apologise. Then renegotiate the original agreement to cover such emergencies.

5 If you are only seeking to modify your agreement slightly, your renegotiation may be as simple as setting the stage and considering other options – Paul and Mary agreed on a destination for their holiday, but Paul later became concerned about the cost and wanted to consider reducing expenses. They decided on a less expensive hotel in a few minutes.

6 If the agreement you want to renegotiate is a basic or long-standing one, you may need to follow the negotiation tree from the beginning – when John's retirement became imminent, he and Rose spend considerable time and care in negotiating their new arrangement to accommodate his retirement to Rose's new career.

The co-operative problem solving process doesn't just end with formalising your decision. Instead, completing your negotiation takes another, and equally vital, step – to celebrate what you have both accomplished by working together to solve your problem.

CELEBRATION

Celebrating the successful completion of your co-operative negotiation accomplished many things. It:

- acknowledges and establishes in your minds that you've accomplished a satisfying end to what may have been a difficult problem;
- helps you focus on the good feelings you have about each other;
- produces what psychologists call a sense of 'closure' – a clear concluding moment, a feeling of resolution to your diligent work, so that there are no residual, unresolved thoughts or feelings as you proceed to your next task;
- makes you focus attention on the positive result of your negotiation;
- provides a moment of warmth and goodwill;

- is a reward for work well done and also creates motivation for future co-operative negotiation.

Most people have a tendency to give more attention to what *doesn't* work than what *does* work and so they never give themselves a chance to acknowledge and savour success. If you do this, you gain no sense of your accomplishments and only become aware of what you feel you *can't* do. You then see yourselves as failures and your relationship as a struggle and you can become discouraged enough to give up. The more difficult the problem you have just solved, the greater the tendency to see negotiation as hard work, and the more important it is to counteract that by celebrating. If you neglect to celebrate the completion of your co-operative problem solving, you will not be motivated to begin on the next problem that needs to be solved.

On the other hand, when you take the time to celebrate a successful negotiation, you allow yourselves to notice the good things about yourselves and your capacity for accomplishment. While a good co-operative solution is a reward in itself, giving yourselves an extra celebration of your success helps you realise how productive you can be as a couple, affirms the power of your teamwork and acknowledges how much you do right. Following the celebration guidelines will build goodwill between you and make all your interactions more positive and easier.

GUIDELINES FOR CELEBRATION

1 *Suggest a celebration*   End each successful negotiation by saying: 'We did it! Now what do you want to do to celebrate?' By talking about what you need to create a feeling of celebration for both of you, you can quickly design your celebration to fit your accomplishment and have fun.

2 *Create a celebration guide*   Develop a list of the items or activities that really mean celebration to both of you: balloons, champagne or wine, friends or family around, using the best china and glasses, having a barbecue on paper plates, going out somewhere nice to eat, having a pizza delivered, buying tickets to a show, going to the cinema, giving each other presents, making love, calling someone to share the good news or just quietly congratulating each other on a job well done. Over a period of time together you can develop a list of celebration items and activities that you can use as a resource each time you want to celebrate a successful negotiation.

   Paul and Mary celebrated their decision by hugging and sending out for a pizza at the end of their negotiation and then, at a special dinner during their holiday, they made a champagne toast to each other for being such clever negotiators. When they came home they also told their friends about how they had the best time of their lives and that negotiation had helped them accomplish it.

   Paul and Carol celebrated their decision to experiment with a cleaner by eating take-away food on paper plates and throwing them away, so no one had to do any dishes.

John and Rose celebrated by making love and telling each other how much they
appreciated their mutual caring and their communication.

You and your partner now have the basic tools you need for co-creating your ideal relationship.
Because these skills, techniques and attitudes are new and somewhat revolutionary compared to
the way most people think relationships work, you will need to practise them. As you would with
any new techniques, start with simple problems, such as who takes out the rubbish bin or what the
schedule for using the bathroom will be. Starting with simple problems gives you the greatest
chance of success and time to practise before you handle more difficult issues. As your familiarity
with co-operative negotiation increases, you will be able to handle more difficult problems. Like
most couples your skills will eventually improve until you can handle your most emotional
disagreements and complex problems without resorting to arguing or fighting.

Once you have sufficient practice, if a problem comes up that you cannot handle through co-
operative problem solving, you'll know that you need an independent outside expert, such as a
marriage counsellor, to help, and the attempts you made at solving the problem co-operatively will
save you time and money in counselling by clarifying where and how you are 'stuck'.

Being skilled in co-operative negotiation makes it possible to work out anything that troubles
you, and even things that don't. With the changes you can make using these techniques, your way
of being together will begin to take on a degree of comfort that feels good for both of you – your
relationship will be satisfying and sustainable and you will be on your way to being equal partners.

The final chapter will show you how, once the day-to-day problems are solved, you can use co-
operative problem solving to shape and create a truly sustainable partnership that is tailor-made to
your individual personalities and meets the needs of both of you to a degree you may not have
dreamed possible.

CHAPTER 7

CREATING EQUAL PARTNERSHIP

Once you have mastered co-operative problem solving you have a proven method you can use together to solve problems, resolve disputes and end conflicts – with the result that you both feel positive about yourselves, each other and your ability to resolve difficult issues together.

What's more important, you now know that it is possible (and you have a method) for both of you to get what you want all the time, every time.

If you are like most couples, the areas where you will find yourselves experiencing the greatest number of problems will be:

- *Romance* Expectations of reproducing the attractive, dramatic and 'perfect' results we see in films and television known as 'romance' can lead us to setting up ideals that are impossible to attain. This creates inevitable disillusionment and a sense of failure.
- *Lovemaking* In a society where sexuality is both suppressed and overexaggerated and where the models presented in fiction are almost always based on the excitement of first love, couples often have no idea how sexuality works in long-term, committed relationships, or how to keep their sexual excitement alive.
- *Personality quirks* All of us have individual behaviours and needs that vary from what our partners were brought up to believe were acceptable and these can produce major struggles when we do not know how to effectively resolve and solve conflicts.
- *Good times and bad times* The natural ups and downs of life, such as illness, financial stress, major business success or parenting issues, have a strong impact on your relationship; those who do not know how to handle the down times often do not know how to handle the good times either.
- *Transitions* Moving gracefully through the years and from one stage of life to another, does not always come naturally. Often when we are struggling with these transitions, we seem to find ourselves in incompatible modes, which lead to conflict and disagreement.
- *Forgiveness* No two people can spend extended time together without making mistakes, hurting feelings or making each other angry. If we do not know how to set these feelings aside and forgive ourselves and our partner, this anger festers and grows until it smothers the

fires of love that brought us together and ends the relationship.

- *Challenges*   Many of us have old, unresolved pain from childhood events or past relationships. These unhealed emotional wounds can cause us to overreact to the normal relationship problems and challenges of life. Such feelings can be overwhelmingly negative and make the problem seem unsolvable, causing serious relationship damage.
- *Unrealistic limitations*   We are just as apt to be unrealistic in believing what we *cannot* do as we are in expecting our selves to do too much; when we believe we can't, we often don't try or give up too easily and prevent ourselves from getting what we really want.

All of these barriers to sustainable equal partnership can be overcome using the skills of co-operative problem solving. As a couple, you become equal partners by honouring each other's personalities, emotional needs, circumstances (such as family situations, financial realities, career demands and the needs of children), individual quirks, foibles, faults and problems. The steps of the negotiation tree ensure that you have methods of confronting and overcoming all these factors when you work together to solve the related problems.

ROMANCE

When you commit yourself to your relationship and live together for an extended period of time, the initial excitement and newness eventually wears off. The heightened energy and excitement of being together, which we call 'romance', lessens when you begin to get into a familiar day-to-day routine. When you live separately every moment spent together is special and it's easy to feel romantic. From the moment you begin to live together, such romantic moments are no longer automatic. Instead, much of your time together is spent on more mundane things, such as doing washing, washing dishes, paying bills or going to work. As soon as the initial newness of living together wears off, such everyday things cease to feel exciting and romantic and you may find yourself feeling worried that your partner no longer cares as much or is as excited to be with you.

Romance is a lovely diversion but it's not a way of life. While romance involves a lot of fantasy, love is grounded in reality. Love requires real people who can be there to support each other through disheartening periods (grief, upsets, financial setbacks) and who can share the joy from triumphs great and small.

Viewed this way, romance becomes a very useful tool you can use to renew the energy in your relationship, whenever you feel the need. By using the negotiation tree to solve the problem of lack of romance or excitement between you, you can create events and rituals that celebrate your love, affection and desire for each other, which will remind and reassure both of you that you are special to each other. These romantic events include:

- arranging a date, a present, a surprise, a joke or a hug when your emotional connection needs reinforcement;
- acting out fantasies: photographer and model, film star couple, nurse and doctor, stripper and audience member;
- taking a special holiday to a romantic spot together;
- setting aside one evening a week for a 'date' and doing what you used to do when you first met;
- spending a weekend morning having breakfast in bed;
- sending a card, a plant, flowers, perfume or other present by messenger or leaving them as a surprise on a day that's not normally a gift-giving occasion;
- taking a class together in something new and fun or getting involved in a voluntary project to create new experiences together.

The possibilities are endless and these romantic boosts to your relationship can keep it from becoming dull or routine. Because what feels romantic and loving to you may or may not be similarly effective for your partner, and vice versa, use co-operative problem solving to develop the romantic ideas that will satisfy both of you. The exercises that will be most helpful here are *clarifying your wants* (page 109), the *abundance worksheet* (page 125), *guidelines for doing research* (page 129) and *guidelines for celebration* page 137).

LOVEMAKING

Most partners who have been together for a while find that their lovemaking changes and is different from when they first met, when their passion grew out of the excitement of the new and unknown. As your affectionate love for your partner deepens, sex may lose some of its raw passion. At the same time there are many benefits to a more emotionally intimate kind of sexual connection.

If you use co-operative problem solving to meet both your needs as your relationship deepens, rather than holding to rigid expectations or getting stuck in repetitive patterns, you will allow your lovemaking to change and grow, as your partnership does.

By using the negotiation tree you can create solutions for lovemaking under all sorts of conditions:

- 'quickies' (sex in a rush);
- sneaky sex (getting around children, in-laws, nosey neighbours);
- romantic sex (for special occasions);
- newlywed sex (the way you used to do it);
- making-up sex (after a disagreement is solved);

- comforting sex (when one of you is sad or stressed);
- relaxing sex (slow, lazy, no pressure);
- reassuring sex (affection and intimacy intended to reassure a partner who is temporarily insecure, or for reaffirming your mutual interest);
- fantasy sex (playacting, dressing up, etc.).

The possible varieties of sexual attitudes, environments, energies and activities are truly endless. A significant part of passion is the exploration of the unknown, and (even when you've been together for many years) there can *still* be an unknown to explore if you approach each other as interesting, growing and changing people and work together to meet your changing needs. The new solutions you create can keep your excitement and passion alive for a lifetime. Co-operative problem solving will help keep you from getting stuck in any one pattern, and allow you an exciting variety of sexual expression. Co-operation creates an attitude of openness to what is happening right now, and responsiveness to each other and the moment, reminiscent of the way you approached lovemaking when you were new to each other.

PERSONALITY QUIRKS

Because we are all different from one another, with different backgrounds, experience and early training, each of us has small quirks, personality traits or habits that must be accommodated, in one way or another, if we wish to have a sustainable relationship. These quirks (a laugh that grates on your nerves, differences in messiness or neatness, irritating jokes or stories, incompatible work schedules, different ideas about housekeeping, your partner's nailbiting or smoking, what and when to feed the dog, how to speak to your children, how warm the room should be), when endured for months and years, can feel like sufficient reason to get a divorce or even attack your partner physically. Many of these things may seem silly and so insignificant that you feel embarrassed to be so unhappy about them, but if you and your partner can't negotiate and resolve your frustration, small irritations can create enough resentment over time to become serious problems.

When such small irritations happen, there are four things you can do:

1 Sometimes, your partner's quirks, such as being messy, picking teeth, not putting lids back on jars tightly, watching too much television or singing off key are small enough to be easily dismissed by deciding that the sum total of your partner more than makes up for the little annoying habits. If you can do this without resentment, your partner's quirks will cease to be a problem.

2 You can also voluntarily modify your own behaviour (go to the bathroom to pick teeth, screw the lids on tight) to reduce the annoyance to your partner.

3 You can minimise (by leaving the room or distracting yourself with a project) the impact of your partner's habits on yourself.

4 If the above three steps don't work, and you feel irritated and resentful about a quirk or habit, you and your partner can use the negotiation tree to discuss the problem objectively, without blame or defensiveness, to create solutions that satisfy both of you.

By using these options, over time, you can create new ways to be partners for a lifetime without getting on each other's nerves.

GOOD TIMES, BAD TIMES

Although we all know that relationships go through good times and bad times, and that as partners we'll probably face fights, tragedies, betrayals and struggles in a lifetime of living together, most people in new relationships (especially those who are in first-time relationships) want very much to believe that they will live 'happily every after'. Hence, they avoid facing the more difficult issues: What happens if you lose your job? How are we going to handle it if we have money difficulties? What if one of us is very sick? What if you are much more successful at your career than I am at mine? What if we become more successful than we ever dreamed? And, often, when life is either very good or very difficult, they don't feel prepared to handle it.

In a lifetime of living together, you and your partner need to be able to handle many ups and downs:

- problems to solve and victories to celebrate;
- moments of excitement and moments of peace;
- times of boredom and times of stressful activity;
- peaks of tremendous love and caring for each other and troughs of distance and irritation;
- fights and harmonious times;
- tragedies and happy events.

By knowing how to use co-operative problem solving you can be prepared to meet all these ups and downs as a team, work together to solve the problems and celebrate your successes. Each experience you have that demonstrates that you are a team and can remain calm in times of crisis, think problems through carefully, solve them in a way that satisfies both of you and enjoy your successes to the fullest will strengthen your bond of trust and partnership and cause you to feel more like equal partners.

TRANSITIONS

As you grow older and gain more experience, your attitudes, expectations and preferences change. Because your relationship is a reflection of the attitudes and experience of both of you, it must change as you do to be sustainable. These continuous changes, whether caused by circumstances (a new job means you must move to a new city), personal growth (you become more self-assured and want to make some new friends or develop a talent) or an unexpected event (your spouse gets a serious illness) always create some turmoil and confusion.

Many couples begin to struggle, compete or fight when this happens, because one or both partners become insecure or frightened when their familiar way of doing things begins to change. When you know co-operative problem solving, however, these transitions can become just a series of problems you must solve. When John and Rose made the transition to John's retirement, they faced many new problems:

- how their finances would change on John's fixed retirement income;
- what John would do to keep active and involved now that he had a lot of unstructured time and felt useless and lost;
- whether to stay in their large house (designed to bring up children in) or sell it and move;
- what limits to set on baby-sitting for their grandchildren;
- how Rose's new career would be affected by John's retirement;
- how much travelling they would do together, where, and in what way.

By solving each of these problems individually rather than letting themselves see the whole thing as one big retirement problem, John and Rose were able to work out a balance between her career and his retirement that allowed them both to feel active and useful, while still allowing them to enjoy leisure time and travelling.

You and your relationship will continue to grow and change and you won't always progress neatly from one stage to the next or find an arrangement that is permanently satisfying. Each of you can even be at different stages at the same time! But, if you use the negotiation tree to help you work out the confusion of new ways of doing things and work together to bridge the differences when they come up, you'll soon learn to see each transition as an exciting new adventure or challenge instead of a frightening change.

FORGIVENESS

In a lifetime of living together, we are bound to hurt each other's feelings, betray trust or let each other down from time to time, usually without intending to. Some emotional hurts, such as when harsh words are spoken in anger and frustration or when an illicit affair occurs during a relationship crisis, will only be resolved through healing and forgiveness. Co-operative problem solving helps us forgive because once we find a solution to the problem that originally caused the hurt, it is much easier to let go of the hurt feelings and get back on good terms with each other.

If you find you are holding hurt, anger or resentment towards your partner, first use the *problem inventory* exercise in chapter 2 (page 25) until you understand clearly enough to communicate what the problem is that needs to be resolved. Then proceed to solve whatever you feel hurt or angry about as if it were any other problem. You'll find that once the problem is solved to your satisfaction, forgiving your partner (and yourself) is made easier by the reassuring knowledge that the problem won't be repeated.

CHALLENGES

*E*very relationship carries challenges to heal and grow and because you and your partner are so intimately involved, your relationship is automatically an environment where old hurts and wounds from the past will arise. In fact, we often challenge each other in the very areas where we are wounded and most need to heal. It is common for couples with corresponding unfinished issues to get together (a woman with an alcoholic father falls for a heavy drinker, a man whose mother was absent or distant is attracted to cold, withdrawn women). When that happens, intimate, committed relationships become arenas for facilitating healing and growth. If painful events happened in your childhood, such as physical or verbal abuse, incest, rape, the loss or death of a parent or sibling, or a severe injury or illness, a relatively mild incident could cause you to unexpectedly relive the pain of your early trauma. Partners who have had very painful past relationships (battering, cheating, lying, being left without warning, severe financial damage) can also carry unhealed psychological wounds which may cause them to overreact to unrelated problems in a current relationship. No matter how loving you are, as partners you can unintentionally recreate old, painful scenes from childhood or previous relationships, which become challenges you must overcome if you don't want this relationship to contain the same problems as those old relationships. The following guidelines will help you.

CHALLENGE INDICATOR CHECKLIST

If you or your partner are over-reacting to the problems because of old, unresolved hurt and trauma from childhood or a past relationship, you will see one or more of the following indicators:

- You can't or won't discuss a particular topic, such as a gambling problem, a difficult in-law, sexual dissatisfaction or disciplining the children.

- A problem seems unsolvable or repeats itself, such as a partner's unreliability or lateness, a struggle over money, or jealousy.
- You argue about different topics but all arguments sound, feel and end the same, for example you both shout until one of you storms out or you don't speak for days.
- You can't negotiate about a particular topic because you end up arguing.
- One of you makes accusations including the words 'you always' or 'you never', indicating stored frustration, resentment and anger about something the other does or doesn't do.
- You feel highly critical, hopeless, angry or resentful about your partner's traits, such as laziness, perfectionism or lateness, or you become obsessed with making your partner see his or her 'problem' and change it.

GUIDELINES FOR OVERCOMING CHALLENGES

If any of the above indicators apply to your situation, you are probably facing a challenge in your relationship and whenever you feel it is threatening to disrupt or destroy your partnership, you can use the following steps to overcome it:

1 *Don't panic*   As painful and overwhelming as they may seem, challenges are common in relationships and can be overcome with co-operative problem solving. Do your best to stay calm and use your active listening skills and attentive speaking skills to find out as much as you can about what the problem is, and follow the negotiation tree as you would with any problem. If you can't stay calm enough, go to Step 5.

2 *Develop temporary solutions*   Use the *guidelines for doing research* (page 129) to develop temporary solutions (such as agreeing to take a break when issues get too heated) while you work separately (using the *setting aside held hurt and anger* exercise (on page 98) or see a psychotherapist) on resolving the trauma or wounds from the past that are evoked by situations in your relationship.

3 *Be as supportive as you can*   If your partner is working on a challenge issue, do your best to be emotionally positive and encouraging. Reassure each other that you won't go away or avoid the issue. If the issue creates problems so difficult (violent outbursts, alcohol or drug addiction, severe sexual problems, emotional breakdowns) that you have to separate to protect yourself, you can still let your partner know you'd be willing to resume the relationship once the problem is handled.

4 *Get outside support*   Develop friends who can support you both emotionally while you overcome the challenge and don't hesitate to let them know when you need help. Having someone who cares and who can listen and support without interferring, will relieve some stress and help you stay calm so you can use your co-operative problem solving skills.

5 *Get professional help*   If you have used the above four steps and co-operative problem solving and the problem still seems overwhelming, especially if one or both of you has a history of

abuse, depression, alcohol problems, rape or incest, get professional help. A therapist is expert in just such issues and can give you the objective, supportive feedback you need to help you to untangle feelings, often unconscious, from the past which affect the present. See the appendix at the back of this book for addresses and telephone numbers of organisations which may be able to help you.

Understanding the signs that indicate challenges, knowing that they exist to varying degrees in most relationships, learning to take care of yourself, recognising that challenges present an opportunity to heal and grow and knowing when to get help will increase your ability to overcome challenges and keep them from permanently damaging your partnership. Challenges are another form of crisis that, when overcome through working together, strengthen your bond of confidence and trust in each other and in your partnership.

UNREALISTIC LIMITATIONS

Most couples who are not satisfied in their relationship have given in to unrealistic limitations. They are limited by false beliefs, 'shoulds', others' expectations or their own lack of experience. Because co-operative problem solving is designed to help you develop new, previously unrealised ideas and solutions for problems, it is the perfect way to overcome unrealistic limitations. Equal partnerships are based on the belief that both of you can get exactly what you want, all the time, based on a profound respect for your individuality and an effort to create and maintain a loving partnership that allows for that individuality; they are based on working together to negotiate a relationship that suits you and your partner, whether traditional, modern or radically different. Equal partnerships are not founded on the form of the relationship, but the content – the emotional satisfaction and practical workability of a relationship that suits the people within it and makes them feel as though they are a supportive and connected team.

As equal partners, you can do anything you both agree on, anything that you are capable of doing. You can live apart but have a committed relationship, you can have two careers and still raise children, you can be a happy family with no children, you can switch traditional gender roles (for example, the man can stay home and look after the children while the woman earns the money), you can be single parents who bring children together to form successful step families, you can live together and be celibate, monogamous or have a sexually open relationship, you can own your own business and work from home.

The whole point of having a mutual, co-operative partnership is to be able to do what works for you. The co-operative negotiation and communication skills you have learned here can help you create any relationship you wish, provided both you and your partner are happy with the results. To overcome unnecessary limitations, you can use the *clarifying wants* exercise in chapter 5 and the *abundance worksheet* and the *brainstorming* exercises in chapter 6 to help you manage everything you want to do and be together, and then use co-operative problem solving to work out how to do it.

As you begin to eliminate these sources of struggle from the relationship, you will know you are on the way to becoming equal partners, because you will experience the rewards:

- you feel supported by each other;
- you always have help and companionship during hard times;
- you know most of the advantages and reasons you are together;
- you have goals to work towards and mutual successes to celebrate;
- when either of you experiences difficulties or failures, you receive solace and reassurance;
- you feel empowered, because two people pulling together have more power than two people pulling separately;
- you have the strength of commitment that comes from knowing that you and your partner are in the best relationship possible for each of you;
- you have the freedom to let your partnership take any form you and your partner want to give it;
- and best of all, your way of being together and your personal wants and needs are flexible enough to change over time as you as individuals change and grow.

Co-operative problem solving is a basic tool that you and your partner can use to renegotiate and modify your relationship to suit your individual changing circumstances as your experience of life changes your attitude and priorities.

By renegotiating each new situation as equal partners, you find you are creating a relationship that changes and grows with you, rather than one that is stagnating and beginning to confine one or both of you.

Ultimately, you will find that you have negotiated your way to a relationship that is unique: it does not look like anyone else's and is custom-made to the specifications of you and your partner, who are unlike anyone else.

As you grow together in this process you may find yourself willing to accept and try new ways of being together that would never have occurred to you before learning to brainstorm to find new solutions that satisfy your wants.

John and Rose had adapted to the traditional relationship model their parents had felt comfortable with: John went to work and earned the money and Rose took care of the house and the children. This worked well for them until the children grew up.

Then, suddenly, their old relationship focus changed and Rose felt lost, unneeded and dissatisfied. But, in following the steps of the negotiation tree, Rose and John explored the problem, uncovered 'shoulds' and rules that were limiting them both, decided to try something different and agreed that Rose would study as a mature student. Her education led to her starting a new career as John approached retirement and their new style of relationship, which ultimately was very enjoyable for both of them, was completely unlike any other relationship they knew.

For Fred and Naomi it was a two-step process: first they had to accept that they both had differing levels of sexual energy and then they both had to accept the startling idea that it was all right for Fred to give himself pleasure at times when Naomi simply was not sexually interested. Before using the negotiation tree, neither of them would have considered such an alternative.

Don and Peter found that, as job and financial circumstances changed, they needed more room and separate office space for Don's business, which meant their financial arrangement had to change. They kept using co-operative problem solving over the years as Don's business grew, until his company filled an entire office building and supported them both in style.

Like these couples, through learning and following the steps of co-operative problem solving, you will create a relationship that suits both the realities of your life and your individual needs and differences.

GOAL SETTING ENHANCES EQUAL PARTNERSHIP

Partners sometimes hesitate to discuss their hopes and dreams because they are afraid that their differences are basically incompatible, and therefore insurmountable, and sharing a vision of the future seems futile. However, when you have mastered co-operative problem solving, you can resolve your differences as partners working together and you will discover that accommodating divergent goals, overcoming the barriers to equal partnership and creating unique solutions to satisfy your wants deepens your bond and commitment and adds zest to your partnership.

Equal partners create a shared sense of purpose by setting relationship goals. When you have a clear vision of your personal and relationship goals all your mutual decisions can be made with your overall goals in mind. By working together to discover your mutual goals, you will gain a deeper understanding of your own as well as your partner's hopes and dreams and the process of setting those goals together will help you know each other better. The love and mutual support you demonstrate to each other when you use your co-operative problem solving skills over the years becomes your equal partnership foundation, free from held anger, resentment and hurt. Love and mutual support reassure you in difficult times and make your joyful times more satisfying.

As equal partners, you can set:

- emotional goals (to make time together more fun and loving, to share feelings more often);
- financial goals (to save to buy a house);
- time goals (to have more time alone together);

149

- health goals (to go to the gym together three times a week, to eat a better diet);
- sexual goals (to make time for sex at least twice a week, to experiment more);
- career goals (to allow one of you to study, to start a business together);
- social goals (to make some new friends, to help the homeless);
- recreational goals (to go on holiday, to relax more at weekends).

In short, whenever you have wishes that are not yet the reality in your relationship, you can set goals to make your wishes come true by using the guidelines that follow.

GUIDELINES FOR SETTING PARTNERSHIP GOALS

To set your equal partnership goals, begin by using the *clarifying you wants* exercise (page 109) until your wishes are clear and easy to communicate, and if your wants are different, use co-operative problem solving to find a workable, mutually satisfying purpose you wish to accomplish. Then follow these steps:

1 *Set your intention* Once you know what you want, you need to agree to go for it. The combination of wanting something and being determined to accomplish it gives you the direction and energy to act on your own behalf. Using the *confirm your decision* step of co-operative problem solving (chapter 6) will help you make sure your intention is mutual.

2 *Break your purpose down* Analyse your purpose into small steps that are feasible to work on, and list them. For example, if your wish was to have a higher education, you could break that down into steps such as: (1) go to library and look up courses to find three possibilities; (2) apply to all of them; (3) apply for grants; (4) enroll for a degree course.

3 *Decide who will do which steps* If it is not immediately obvious, use co-operative problem solving to decide who does which steps. In the process of negotiating, you may find that the experience and expertise you gain as you work together will change either the steps or your stated purpose a bit, as it does in any experiment. Those changes are part of the learning process of setting goals and carrying them out.

4 *Do something* Obviously, you won't achieve your goal if you never get around to doing anything. Breaking your goal down into small steps should help you feel less overwhelmed and more motivated. However, if you find that you are not doing what you agreed to, go back to Guideline 2 and break the goal into smaller, easier steps or use your active listening and attentive speaking skills (pages 53–54) to find out what is in the way.

5 *Celebrate what you've accomplished* Use the *guidelines for celebration* (page 137) to celebrate every step you complete, to keep your enthusiasm high and create motivation.

By setting your intention, creating small steps and completing and celebrating each step of your plan as you go along, you'll find that you have changed your relationship in the desirable ways you want and that even the work of creating change has been fun. After a few goal-setting successes, you'll find that your sense of commitment and confidence in your equal partnership grows stronger. Your equal partnership will meet your needs so well and will be so comfortable and suitable for both of you that there is no motivation to leave and every incentive to stay. In this way, creating an equal partnership is a by-product of seeking your mutual satisfaction through co-operative problem solving.

Such a relationship is sustainable and lasting because it contains none of the problems that cause most relationships to break up. Instead of fighting, you work together; instead of feeling deprived, both of you feel fulfilled; instead of frustration, you find solutions; instead of defeat you experience success.

In short, equal partners have a sustainable relationship for the following reason: why would anyone want to leave a relationship in which they get what they want all the time, even if their wants change as the years go by?

Co-operation and negotiation are powerful tools because they are completely flexible and applicable to almost any possible relationship situation. By learning to use them well, you'll be doing the most you can do to guarantee the success of your equal partnership and you will maximise your pleasure in your relationship and in your lives together.

Useful Addresses

BRITISH ASSOCIATION FOR COUNSELLING
1 Regent Place
RUGBY CV21 2PJ
0788 578328

BRITISH ASSOCIATION OF PSYCHOTHERAPISTS
37 Mapesbury Road
LONDON NW2 4HJ
081 452 9823

INSTITUTE OF FAMILY THERAPY
43 New Cavendish Street
LONDON W1M TRG
071 935 1651

INSTITUTE OF MARITAL STUDIES
120 Belsize Lane
LONDON NW3 5BA
081 435 7111

KARNAC BOOKS
118 Finchley Road
LONDON NW3 5HJ
071 431 1075
and
58 Gloucester Road
LONDON SW7 4QY
071 584 3303

RELATE MARRIAGE GUIDANCE
(London Office)
76a New Cavendish Street
London W1M 7LB
071 580 1087

TAVISTOCK CENTRE
120 Belsize Lane
LONDON NW3 5BA
071 435 7111

About The Authors

Tina B. Tessina, Ph.D., Licensed Marriage Family Therapist, has been helping individuals and couples improve their lives and relationships for fifteen years. Dr Tessina lectures throughout the US at academic and professional conferences and is a frequent guest on national and local television and radio programmes. Her previous books include *How to Be a Couple and Still Be Free; Lovestyles: How to Celebrate Your Differences; Gay Relationships: How to Find Them, How to Improve Them, How to Make Them Last*; and *The Real Thirteenth Step: Discovering Confidence, Self-Reliance and Autonomy Beyond the Twelve Step Programs*.

Riley K. Smith, M.A., is a Licensed Marriage and Family Therapist who has been helping couples and individuals create lasting, satisfying relationships since 1976. He lectures and teaches classes and workshops in addition to his psychotherapy practice. He is co-author, with Dr Tessina, of *How to Be a Couple and Still Be Free*.

Jill Curtis, M.B.A.P., is the Psychotherapy Editorial Consultant to Headway. She is a Training Therapist and Supervisor and works full-time as a psychoanalytic psychotherapist in private practice in London.

Acknowledgements

FOR TINA TESSINA

Riley K Smith, for co-operative problem solving above and beyond the call of duty; and for letting the best book possible be more important than anything else. Richard Sharrard, as always, for living the attitudes set forth here, and for being my primary support, encouragement, and team member. Jeremy P. Tarcher, for his continued support and encouragement. It's a privilege to work with him. My editor and friend, Jean Stine, who has taught me more than my B.A., M.A., and Ph.D. put together. Denton Roberts, M.Div, MFCC, who gave me the training and the encouragement to be effective and original in my work and my ideas. My support team, who continue to encourage me and distract me when I need it, though they all must be sick of this by now: Maggie and Eddie Bialack, Joan and Bill Mueller, Sylvia and Glen McWilliams, Ron Creager, Isadora Alman, Mike Miller, Larry Kern and Elliott Stoughton, and the 'Beach, Beach, Beach' salon. Fellow writers Isadora Alman, Arno Karlen, and Warren Farrell, who have been generous with their support and guidance. Glen and Richard, computer whizzes, who came to my rescue several times. To my secretary, Ruth Campbell, for her calm, competent work, which makes my work easier. All my clients, who are the primary resource of everything I have learned, and who make my work a joy.

FOR RILEY K. SMITH

I started my adult life believing that because I alone am responsible for my life I had to do my life alone. Developing and working with the material in this book was a part of my learning that, although I'm responsible, I don't have to do it alone. I want to acknowledge with love and appreciation a few of the key members of the team that created *Equal Partners*: Tina Tessina, my long-time friend and colleague, who shared in the creation of this material and who patiently taught me a new way to write. Rhoda Pregerson, who has practised being Equal Partners with me since 1985. Jean Stine, the editor who put our thoughts in order and made a book out of them. Jeremy Tarcher, the publisher who believed the book worthy of his investment. Al Saunders, who got us started by publishing the early version of this material. The editorial and production staff of J. P. Tarcher and G. P. Putnam, including Daniel Malvin, editor, Susan Shankin, art director at Tarcher, and Coral Tysliava, copy chief, Timothy Meyer, copy editor, at Putnam, and Mauna Eichner, text designer.